FROM CELLMATES TO SOULMATES

INTEGRATING SALES AND SERVICE

MARK W. HEISLER

SUZANNE BALDINO JONES

"From CellMates to SoulMates: Integrating Sales and Service," by Mark W. Heisler and Suzanne Baldino Jones. ISBN 1-58939-339-2(softcover). 1-58939-340-6 (hardcover).

Cover designed by Robert Michael Communications, Inc.

Library of Congress Number on file with the publisher and authors.

Published 2002 by Virtualbookworm.com Publishing Inc., P.O. Box 9949, College Station, TX , 77842, US. ©2002 Mark W. Heisler and Suzanne Baldino Jones. All rights reserved. No part of this publication may be reproduced, stored in a retrieval system, or transmitted in any form or by any means, electronic, mechanical, recording or otherwise, without the prior written permission of Mark W. Heisler and Suzanne Baldino Jones.

Manufactured in the United States of America.

DEDICATION

To our "enduring afterglow…" our children:
Anthony, Douglas and Morgan

ACKNOWLEDGEMENTS

From CellMates to SoulMates: Integrating Sales and Service is a dream come true for both of us. Writing *CellMates to SoulMates* has been a wonderful and exciting challenge. In many respects, the development of the book is a microcosm of our relationship: 50/50 partnerships are like that. Since founding our consulting firm, the Competitive Business Strategy Group (CBSG), we share the same goals. Over the years, we have come to realize that goals alone are not enough to sustain a relationship. We communicate — with passion and purpose — about everything. We talk, confer, brainstorm, debate, and argue. In the end, we ultimately agree to the ideas and solutions outlined in the book. *CellMates to SoulMates* is so much a part of who we are that neither one of us remembers who originally came up with a particular concept. We also work at our partnership continuously. [It's part of our quest to self-actualize]. Thankfully, we continue to take each other's character flaws and idiosyncrasies in stride. The mutual trust and respect we share for one another has blossomed into a collaboration that is beyond words.

We are blessed with the love, support and talents of so many people who made *CellMates to SoulMates* possible. First, we must thank our spouses Karen and David. The sacrifices you made over the years demonstrate your love for us, and the confidence you share in our collective abilities. To our kids, Anthony, Doug and Morgan, you are always there to keep us delightfully focused on everything that's truly important in life. To our parents, you loved us unconditionally, even when we didn't deserve it. You shaped us into the people we are today.

To the members of our Business Advisory Board, Robert Colleluori, Tom Forst, Gene Preston, Marikay Swartz, David Scheuring and Bob Tallon, thank you for your reasoned and sensible advice and your unwavering belief in us and our work. Without your pushing and prodding, this book would still be a collection of ideas locked somewhere in the deep recesses of our brains. Each of you contributed greatly to our personal and professional growth.

Our unconditional gratitude goes to friend and editor Mark Speeney. Mark, you helped us take our words and ideas to another level. Your feedback was always constructive and never judgmental, the perfect mix for two strongly opinionated people.

There are so many other wonderful friends and colleagues who made valuable contributions to this book. To Robert and friends at Robert Michael Communications, thank you for your talents and your patience. Thank you Bobby Bernshausen at Virtualbookworm.com for such a great job. To our technical gurus, Glenn Fennimore from Just Cause Video as well as Erin Blackwell, our Internet maven: thank you for using your many techno savvy skills on our behalf.

We are also very fortunate to work with so many clients who trusted us, listened to our advice, and even suspended disbelief long enough for us to test out a new idea. Every client experience contributed to this body of work. Consulting is a tough business, because you're only as good as your last client assignment. The only positive feedback one gets is when a client rehires you or recommends you to someone else. We are extremely proud of the fact that every one of our clients has either rehired or referred us.

Last, but surely not least, we must tip our hats in gratitude to all the people who tirelessly worked with us on "project teams" over the years. Thank you for making us look good!

TABLE OF CONTENTS

INTRODUCTION

The difficulty lies, not in the new ideas, but in escaping from the old ones...

John Maynard Keynes (The Theory of Employment, Interest and Money, 1936.)

THE BUSINESS OF BUYING AND SELLING

The business of business is buying and selling. Companies pour millions of dollars each year in their "selling" initiatives hoping to draw people into "buying." Let's face it...no matter how businesses package products or develop their sales force; there is no business without customers. The assumption is that so long as companies can attract customers in sufficient numbers the firm will grow and ultimately turn a profit. Retention and loyalty, while viewed as lofty outcomes, are rarely seen as integral to sustaining a healthy bottom line. This traditional attitude is fundamentally flawed. It's our experience that firms who only focus on attracting new customers never achieve their full profit potential, because they don't view keeping customers (or the higher yardstick—customer loyalty) as a requirement for corporate profitability.

One would think that with centuries of experience in trade and commerce to draw upon, and countless books and articles about sales and service, someone would have devised a surefire method for sales initiatives that guarantee long-term customer loyalty and retention. The truth is organizations still struggle with customers. Sales and service, while responsible for the very same customers, don't share the same goals or coordinate work. They barely communicate. Sales and service are solitary, shackled *Cell-Mates* having little in common other than the signature embossed on their respective paychecks.

Through our integration model, sales and service become engaged—learning to work as one—knocking down the institutional walls that divide them. They are transformed into kindred spirits, *SoulMates*; the ensuing improvements to customer acquisition, loyalty and retention cause profits to increase regardless of the economic climate.

3 THINGS YOU OUGHT TO KNOW

Our model for sales and service integration is actually a process for a dramatic "organizational transformation," a paradigm shift that changes an entire company. The three fundamental tenets of integrating sales and service illustrate the required change in mindset:

Sales and service must be:

1. Part of the same continuous process.

2. Everything a company does.

3. Everybody's job.

Figure 1: Tenets for Integrating Sales and Service

Following these three principles unites sales and service into a healthy partnership: two parties sharing goals and a common purpose, continually coming together in order to perpetuate and advance customer relationships. When a

12

company's sales efforts are integrated with its service delivery and execution, sales and service no longer remain mutually exclusive customer deliverables, but instead become extensions of each other. Customer retention and loyalty (and the services built to support them) become natural, integral components of a single sales cycle.

Once a company accepts this combined view of sales and service, the cycle never ends. Business units such as operations and information technology (i.e. the service organization) understand that they perform responsibilities that significantly impact the customer. The organization executes and delivers on the promises made by sales and creates an environment that perpetuates the customer relationship. Sales and service (execution and delivery) becomes everybody's job.

HOW INTEGRATION TOOK ROOT

Our story would have more sex appeal if we said there was a real epiphany that led us to the idea of sales and service integration. The truth is, things just evolved. Here's the abridged version:

Before CBSG, we worked together as executives for a financial services company. Many of our initial insights vis-à-vis integrating sales with service delivery and execution were born from this experience. It didn't take us long to realize that the firm's customers had a poor opinion of the service organization. Customers complained that service could not deliver on the promises being made by the sales division. It was our job to fix the problems and to repair the corporate image.

We implemented a variety of solutions. We improved communication between the service organization, sales and the customer. We modified work processes and restructured management. We changed attitudes toward service. Suzanne used the phrase, "...wrap service around everything you do," as a way to exemplify our vision for a customer-focused, relationship-based business model. In hindsight, there was one major flaw with our efforts. Our efforts were focused primarily on "after-sale" improvement, so any integration that occurred with sales was purely unintentional.

Once out on our own, we observed that many of our clients were having similar issues with customers. In client interviews we heard a common theme: "no matter how effective [our clients'] initial sales efforts are, customers are very quickly discounted and disenfranchised from the organization." There were other signs too: slow sales growth, awful retention rates and little customer loyalty. As staunch conspiracy theorists, we knew intuitively that our clients' experiences were not coincidental. Something was clearly amiss.

Then while designing a new sales program for a technology client, who was changing its core business from a service bureau into a software provider, it finally clicked. All those problems we were seeing weren't just "service" problems after all. They were both sales and service problems! Sales and service didn't communicate with each other unless they had to. Sales and service didn't coordinate work; they saw no reason to. Sales and service used different forms, processes and technology to perform the same activities. As a result of these revelations, we created a program that unified or integrated sales and service around the customer.

We altered the client's organizational structure; we revamped sales and service roles; we changed work processes; and we redesigned technology systems to center activities around customer relationships. The results were undeniable. The business units rallied behind their new world and customers responded accordingly — strong sales, improved retention and a foundation for real loyalty. Sales and service integration was born. Since that time we have continued to test, refine and expand our integration methods with real clients in the corporate trenches.

WHO SHOULD READ THIS BOOK

"Everyone," says our marketing firm. We like to think so too, but realistically, the target audience is executives, business owners, managers and anyone who has aspirations to be one. The book is perfect for the CEO/owner, senior executive and middle manager who wants to create a competitive advantage by repositioning the organization around its customers.

WHAT WE DO

It's a team sport. Consequently, to put integration into practice, we work with all levels of the company. The executive team must analyze the current situation and guide the entire process. We offer them objectivity, options and recommendations on the best course of action to implement. The rest of the organization must understand and buy-in to the value of the program. We train a project team to design integrated work processes and systems. Workshops are conducted to break down barriers between the sales and service silos and to cross-train sales and service employees. As facilitators, we assist management to make the tough implementation decisions that get results.

WHAT TO EXPECT

Before we continue, let's set the record straight. Much has been written of late on topics such as creating customers for life, customer-focused selling, building customer loyalty, and developing customer value. While there is merit to many of the opinions and theories espoused in these materials, the authors tend to focus more on why companies should adopt these stellar ideas, not what to do and how to do it. Even though the reader nods with approval as they turn each page, they quickly conclude that the nuts and bolts to put things into action are missing. We promise not to make the same mistakes.

While *CellMates to SoulMates* is about customer relationship management, it does not describe fuzzy concepts to make customers happy. The end game is to increase profits. The book offers tangible ideas and tools that can be applied across management disciplines to achieve greater profitability through improved customer acquisition, by building customer loyalty and customer retention with a purpose: to cultivate additional sales opportunities (e.g. generating repeat and referral sales as well as recurring revenue streams.) Here are some of the results we have achieved:

- *Increasing profitability* seventeen (17%) percent to thirty (30%) percent in first year
- *Growing new sales* ten (10%) percent to twenty-five (25%) percent annually
- *Expanding repeat and referral sales* with *existing* customer fifteen (15%) percent to forty (40)% percent and a minimum of fifty (50%) percent respectively within two years
- *Increasing customer retention rates* a full five (5) percentage points in six months and achieving a minimum retention rate of ninety (90%) percent in two

two years
- *Reducing structural expenses* within eighteen months; reductions ranged from seven (7%) percent to twelve (12%) percent *(excluding staff)*
- *More efficient cycle times* in less than one year; *customers* benefited from cycle time reductions ranging from twenty (20%) percent to as much as three hundred sixty (360%) percent

As suggested by the book's title, we use a comparative literary device that parallels the stages of the sales and service process to the joys and disappointments, the thrills and the trials of' experiences in personal relationships. Healthy relationships, whether personal or in business, happen when you employ the same ideals. Our book illustrates that by building a partnership between sales and service, the entire organization can develop and maintain healthy relationships with customers.

The first few chapters of the book focus on the organizational DNA that gives birth to poor customer interactions. Chapter 1 examines why businesses develop unhealthy customer relationships. We illustrate how organizations unintentionally push their customer away and into the arms of the competition during what we know as the traditional sales process. Chapter 2 discusses the characteristics and scope of customer retention and loyalty problems in organizations today. We also review management's customary solutions to these retention and loyalty troubles and why those responses are inadequate. Management's multiple personality disorder is the subject of Chapter 3. We describe three systemic organizational behaviors that effectively send mixed messages to employees and customers, ultimately harming internal and external relationships. Once readers understand the organizational dynamics that hurt customer relationships, Chapter 4 explains the key integration concepts that provide the foundation for organizational change. The remainder of the book describes, in detail, the step-by-step methodologies we use to implement the model. In addition to charting the means, we spend a great deal of time discussing matters of "savvy." It's essential, in our opinion, to address the realities of corporate politics surrounding integration. In Chapters 5 and 6 we discuss the strategic direction that senior management must take to align the business around its customers. Breaking down the long-standing barriers between sales and service is the focus of Chapter 7. In rapid-fire succession we deal with the nuts and bolts of integration in Chapters 8 to 10: creating customer-oriented processes and systems; reshaping jobs and structures; and handling the people issues associated with those endeavors.

We have a few final thoughts. We freely confess to using all kinds of attention grabbers—catchy tag lines, memory aids, and even sexual innuendo—just to make a point, but that's as far as it goes. *CellMates to SoulMates* equips the reader with the tools to navigate through the sales and service integration process providing insights derived from working in real companies, with real employees and real customers.

Some of the ideas are "no-brainers": things that can be accomplished easily with little risk to both the implementer and the organization. Take advantage of these opportunities! Other recommendations require one to conduct some additional analysis; to plan, to build consensus, to swallow hard and make the tough decisions that make things happen. Take these challenges. There are no results for those who do nothing; and after all is said and done, it's results that matter most.

CHAPTER 1—THE RITES OF SELLING

There is no more pleasurable orgasm than a rising sales graph...

William Burroughs, US Author

O ver the years we have observed situations where a company's traditional view of sales and service roles and responsibilities (and the internal practices that envelop them) inadvertently sever customer relationships. All the good intentions, regular training and snappy mission statements only focus on loving the customer; the daily activities of a company's sales and service business units nevertheless disengage the customer from the organization. We call these self-inflicted "disconnects" the Stages of Customer Separation.

STAGE 1. THE DATING STAGE

Selling is exhilarating! Sellers love to sell. Buyers are primed to buy. It's like sex. Words can't adequately describe the salesperson's emotional responses: excitement and anxiety, hope and fear, love and desire! Just ask anyone who sells for a living and they'll tell you that they experience all these feelings at one time or another as they navigate through the sales process:

Dressed for success and feeling confident, you're one big nerve ending. The adrenaline is pumping; your palms are sweaty; your heart is beating hard and fast with anticipation. You expectantly scan the room. Your eyes fall on a possible prospect. You slowly look them over evaluating their every move. Your eyes finally meet. You sense a glimmer of interest. You make your move. As you walk toward them you breathe deeply, reminding yourself that you're trained to handle moments just like this. With an extended hand and warm smile you say, "Hi!" They smile in return. You decide it's time to get better acquainted.

You make small talk, searching for common interests. You're on your game—charming, funny, serious— whatever the situation requires. You look into their eyes deeply. You listen. You empathize. You ask probing questions. You tell them you understand their deepest wants and needs...

It's your turn now, so you go with your best stuff. You describe your features, your benefits, how you add value. You clarify and summarize your thoughts—turning them into a cohesive presentation. Time stands still as you wait for the rejection...that never comes.

You both decide to get together again, and again. You anticipate each meeting with an intense combination of excitement and anxiety. You wine, dine, and talk passionately for hours. Even those short handwritten notes and the occasional unexpected call just to say "hello" works like magic. Everything is so new and exciting, so carefree, so fresh and so exhilarating. You can't get enough. You know this one's right. It's tangible—you can feel it!

Things snowball. You tell one another you're the answer to each other's prayers and pledge eternal love and devotion. Before you know it, you're making plans and promises. No more doubts. You're a good match. Everything's ready. Ain't love grand?

So, what does all this talk of dating, love and lust have

to do with a book on sales and service? Why, everything!

The entire business of buying and selling abounds with expressions of love (and lust). Sales people and their companies reap tremendous pleasure and satisfaction from making sales. The degree of ecstasy varies—all sales are **not** created equal; rather, they come in different shapes and sizes. Some sales occur quickly, others require time and patience. Sales can (usually) happen only once, although there are some special examples that can generate multiple occasions. You get the point. On the other side of the transaction, it is assumed customers also find joy and satisfaction when a want or need is fulfilled through the purchase.

When a product or service matches the needs of a customer and the customer is willing to pay for it, everyone wins...the company and the customer begin on a path both parties believe will be a long-term, "loving" relationship. However, it's not just about the exchange of money. This is more than a marriage of convenience. There is an emotional response for both parties, what we call the "newness bias."

We regularly ask sales people, "Do you get the same rush from making a sale to an existing customer as you do when making a sale from a new one?"

As unscientific a response as it may be, they answer with a resounding, "No!" Given the consistent reaction, we get the impression that making a repeat sale is about as exciting as kissing a sibling. Most sales people get their juice from winning over a new customer. Is it any wonder that so many sales people disappear once the client signs on the dotted line?

Now, some may argue that these reactions are part and parcel to a competitive market place. We could buy this argument if this newness bias did not harm an organization's existing customer base and it was localized to the sales force. Just peek under the covers at the way firms construct their sales and marketing initiatives and you'll find that organizations are, as a whole, juiced by new too.

Businesses constantly invent new ways to lure new customers into the fold. Corporations spend billions to make products better, improved, and reformulated and they continually reinvent services to include the latest and greatest bells and whistles. A company's product development efforts, advertising campaigns, and pricing structures are all geared to attract new customers. The telecommunications industry illustrates the point quite well.

Once upon a time, there was a huge corporation that monopolized the entire long distance telephone market. Fast-forward several years and now there are several big national companies and some smaller regional ones too. The market is mature. Telephone service has become a very reliable commodity. There's no significant product differentiation. The major preoccupation of each of these firms is to grab market share by luring new subscribers away from competitors. To do this, the big national long-distance players introduce splashy new service plans. Price is the carrot. However, existing customers need not inquire. If you're a current customer and want a lower cost plan, you are better off signing up with the competition.

Couple these circumstances with nominal customer acquisition costs and low margins and it's no wonder customer service stinks across the telecom spectrum. It's easier to reach a telemarketer than it is to make contact with a live, breathing customer service representative. Phone bills are long, complicated and filled with jargon. [We're convinced it's done in order to intentionally confuse customers so they can't decipher the actual cost of the service]. Nonetheless, so long as net subscribers increase each quarter everything is right with the world.

22

To be fair, businesses shouldn't take the rap for this newness problem alone. Customers also fall in lust and in love all the time. Being obsessed with instant gratification, keeping up with the Jones, or acquiring the latest gadget, is a preoccupation of businesses and retail consumers alike. For example, we've seen more than a few companies spend major money to replace perfectly good software with a new system that appeared to offer an increase in productivity. It didn't matter that the new system required savvy light years beyond the average user's computer competency. The answer to this literacy gap is a training program and luke-warm tech support. Soon after implementation, the users (customers) are frustrated and disenchanted.

Companies, like people, put their best face on when they enter into a relationship with someone new. Not long ago while driving to a client we heard a story on *National Public Radio* where the commentator noted that it takes individuals about six months into a new relationship before they take off their "masks." That's essentially what happens in the sales dating stage; the company puts on its best face and the lust/love dance begins.

Now factor in the competitive nature of sales. The quotas, the contests, or hunger (i.e. a salesperson's need to "put bread on the table") can create a sales environment where a survival instinct takes control. Simply stated, the needs of the salesperson and the organization can override those of the customer. In some it breeds inappropriate or unproductive behaviors:

- Chasing after a sale long past the point of financial viability
- Making promises that can't be delivered
- Setting unrealistic expectations (whether done knowingly or out of ignorance)

23

- Selling solely on price and taking a loss upfront; rationalizing that repeat business will ultimately lead to profit
- Inventing need; using fear tactics that result in manufacturing a sale at all cost

When these things happen, the company and customer are the ultimate losers because the relationship is never on solid ground.

Even in a best customer-dating scenario, when the sales force, the company's sales practices and the customer work to build a healthy customer relationship, they can still become trapped in the next stage of separation.

STAGE 2. THE MORNING AFTER STAGE

You thought this day would never come. You're nervous and excited, just like when you first met. So many sleepless nights fantasizing about what it would be like — all the emotions, all the titillating sensations. You feel this incredible urgency when you enter the room. Now for the moment of truth: you're ready as they take the pen and sign on the deal. What a rush!

> There's nothing better than closing a sale!

With the relationship consummated and the contract in hand, you talk of sunsets and white horses. You're both confident that this storybook relationship will be one for the ages, living blissfully in a perpetual state of "happily ever after." After a night of passion, you wake up the next morning, rubbing the sleep from your eyes. You roll over, and a little voice says, "Oh my God!" "What was I thinking?" You thought you went to bed with Mel Gibson and woke up to find Hannibal Lechter. [For the guys, you went to bed with Julia Roberts and woke up to Lorena Bobbitt]!

The Morning After Stage is set in motion once the deal is signed, sealed and then "delivered," and the customer is handed off to other parts of the organization. In most organizations, the responsibility for the customer shifts from sales to service.

In every sale, the company and/or its sales representatives, makes certain explicit and implicit promises to customers about its product or service. Depending upon the size and complexity of the deal, those promises can be pretty extensive. For the customer's part, they agree to pay consideration for the product or service. Beyond the explicit agreement, both parties also bring along baggage in the form of perceptions, expectations and emotions that can't be ignored. For example, sales people answer questions and respond to issues and objections raised by the prospect; offering descriptions, solutions, opinions, claims, guarantees and sometimes exceptions. These discussions shape the customer's expectations concerning the terms and conditions of the sale.

There is also an emotional connection established during the process. This is true particularly in face-to-face selling. Good sales people make customers feel like they're the only one. The customer, having fallen in love, trusts that the salesperson will take care of them. Consequently, the customer expects the salesperson to remain engaged throughout the life of the relationship. Soon, however, the customer learns differently; they come to realize that they're really part of a twisted "love triangle." Once the agreement is consummated, the salesperson hands-off responsibility for the customer by communicating the terms and conditions of the sale to others in the organization.

The triggering mechanism for the handoff is usually some internal paperwork (i.e. application, purchase order, contract, etc.) or an internal system, which is designed to codify the <u>explicit</u> promises of the sale. Employees in the service organization—those responsible for product or service delivery—receive the communication and perform the work necessary to get the product or service in the hands of the customer.

However, those embedded assurances—the solutions, opinions, etc. that were made while dating—are rarely communicated to those responsible for delivery of the product or service and when the commitments are not delivered, the salesperson becomes the bogeyman. Yet, the salesperson is only partially to blame. They are generally working within the conventional operating environment created by the company. The bad customer handoff is an outgrowth of established corporate sales and service practices.

The organization designs work processes, procedures and systems to communicate and maintain customer needs. The assumption is that the salesperson communicated, through established channels, everything that the service organization needs to fulfill all commitments for the delivery. Never assume.

A few years back we recommended a software application to a client. It was an expensive and complicated arrangement. In addition to the typical installation work, a fair amount of software customization was necessary to fulfill the client's business requirements. During the sales process, the client's specifications were communicated in writing—as were the solutions. Furthermore, there were also a series of sidebar discussions and corresponding answers that were worked out between the client, the salesperson and the technical sales specialist assigned to the case. Some points were formalized in writing; other, less complex issues were worked through orally. Then several weeks later...

With the sale made, a joint implementation team was appointed to customize and install the software. Neither the sales rep nor the technical sales specialist was part of the group; even though the client requested at least one of them remain on the project. "Don't worry, we do this all the time," the software vendor said, "we have great systems and great people to ensure we won't miss a beat." It didn't take long before we found ourselves back to square one, rehashing and repeating issues that we thought were already resolved. Only after the customer threatened to cancel the contract, did the company relent and bring the technical salesperson back on the team. The system was successfully installed, but we estimated it cost the client a quarter million dollars and three months worth of delays. All of this could have been avoided if someone from the original sales team had remained engaged in the process. This story is not an isolated situation. We have witnessed this problem time and time again.

Let's say customer handoffs are flawless; the company's sales and service groups work well together—seamless execution—as we like to say. Customers are content, satisfied, even fulfilled. Ah, the unencumbered bliss of newlyweds. Inevitably, as in all relationships the customer relationship begins to change.

STAGE 3. THE COMPLACENCY STAGE

The honeymoon is now a distant memory, but if you're truly honest with each other, a few "warts" begin to appear. Nothing serious, mind you. "Did she always have that irritating laugh?" "He doesn't understand me." There's now no denying that things have changed; you both realize that only time will tell whether behaviors can improve. Will you see enough value to make the relationship work; or, will you continue to make empty promises? Will mutual respect and trust return; or, will innuendo and suspicions turn to anger? Will you find that special bond again; or, will you conclude there is nothing to work out?

Every relationship, no matter how good at the start, changes with time. In certain relationships, the people mature and grow closer together — through hard work, compromise, sincerity, and a host of other truisms, a delightful harmony and an intense loyalty results. Sadly, other situations move in the opposite direction. Complacency sets in. One or both parties become stagnant and stifled, which ultimately leads to discontentment, and in extreme cases, things can get downright nasty.

Customer relationships work exactly the same. How can something so good turn so bad? Why do so many of these business/customer relationships end in "divorce"?

Companies and customers "fall out of love" at alarming rates: the average business loses twenty (20%) percent of their customer base each year.[1] The reason most customers stop doing business with firms is quite troubling. Surveys consistently indicate that seven (7) out of ten (10) customers defected because they either felt ignored or experienced poor service.[2] That's right, they feel ignored! Think about the last time that you, as a customer, felt ignored or suf-

---

[1] Cannie, Joanne Koob. "Turning Lost Customers into Gold:...and the Art of Achieving Zero Defections." AMACOM. November, 1993.

[2] Fritz, Roger. "Treat Customers Right." Business Journal Raleigh Durham. April 17, 1998. As quoted from an American Quality Control survey conducted to determine why a company loses customers.

fered through a thoughtless service experience. Did you continue to patronize that business? Absolutely not!

It's commonplace for people to wax nostalgic about the good ol' days when customer service meant something. We fondly reminisce about the mom and pop operations where personal attention was standard practice. Everyone knew you by name; knew your likes and dislikes (with no CRM system necessary), threw in a little something extra, and even took credit until payday. You never felt ignored.

It's more than just a feeling; the daily routines of an organization, its processes and systems, can cause customers to leave. Put your customer hat on again and think back to some of your more recent encounters with a company — browsing an Internet site, making a telephone inquiry, reviewing an invoice, or completing paperwork. Did you come away from the experience feeling that the company cared whether the interaction was good for you or not? Chances are you left frustrated and angry because you were forced to interact with forms and technology, procedures and policies developed to serve the internal convenience of those who work with them, rather than the convenience of those affected by them. Our cynicism about this stage is well founded. Consider a few client situations:

- An automated attendant that droned on for three full minutes before a customer heard *all* the options. There were *thirteen* service options in the first menu level alone!
- A new customer application package that contained no less than eight separate forms. The customer's name and address was repeated and required on each.
- The Internet-based "expedited" direct purchasing system that exclusively used internal product

29

codes and operational jargon for the product descriptions. Customers had no idea at what they were looking.

- The new account processing procedures that took an average of thirty business days to complete.

In summary, at each stage of separation, the company's actions (both conscious and unconscious) cause tangible changes to the customer relationship. Sales holds the customer's hand early in the process — taking care of everything along the way. All of a sudden the rules change. Sales leaves to search for the next new conquest and the customer is whisked off to the world of "service" where employees are poorly prepared to perpetuate the relationship sales began. The outcome is always the same — customers leave.

It's a funny thing about companies. Everybody, from those occupying corner offices to the clerks working in the mailroom, says the right things when it concerns customers. Everyone knows how important customers are to the success of a business. Why is it then when customers leave, it's no more than a blip on the company's radar screen?

CHAPTER 2—UNTIL DEATH DO US PART

Nowadays love is a matter of chance, matrimony a matter of money and divorce a matter of course.

*Helen Rowland **(Reflections of a Bachelor Girl, 1903)***

From an early age we are taught "you need to kiss a lot of frogs before you find your prince." We spend years kissing frogs as we search for our prince or princess. Then, we find the "one" or at least we think so... Even when we're certain, the thought of settling down with one person is scary. FOREVER is a mind-numbing notion!

Customer relationships are the same. Customers have many options and are constantly bombarded with information about which products and services they should purchase. In the past, a product or service advantage could differentiate a company for years, which happily made sales and service seem trouble-free. No more. Today, there are lots of unremarkable companies searching for the same customers offering indistinguishable products and services. These competitors can copy and even eclipse a product/service advantage in months, weeks or days. If a customer becomes unsatisfied about something—anything—they show their displeasure by quietly walking away to do business elsewhere. Even worse, companies appear unaffected by these defections.

BUT WE REALLY DO CARE

It's not for lack of trying, caring, or wanting to do what's right by customers. The amount of time, money, and resources organizations pour into sales and service activities speaks volumes. Every business labors with the customer basics—getting customers, keeping them and building loyalty. Unfortunately, small firms to major corporations don't make the grade. Customers still leave. It's not because customers don't have strategic importance.

Consider how companies have aggressively pursued cross-selling and product bundling strategies. For much of the 1990s, executives announced one blockbuster merger/acquisition after another where leveraging existing customers (by providing them with multiple products through one company) was a major reason for the corporate marriage. Media companies and financial service industries in particular touted this strategy. For example, the $82.9 billion merger of Travelers Insurance and Citicorp was in large measure fueled by the desire to cross-sell financial services to one huge customer base. The AT&T/Media One deal was initiated when Jack Armstrong, AT&T's CEO, became enthralled with the idea of providing both long distance telephone and cable television services through one medium of transmittal. Likewise the AOL/Time Warner merger was in part fueled by bringing Time Warner's vast array of media content directly to the computers of millions of AOL subscribers. There is no such thing as a sure thing in the world of mergers and acquisitions. As outsiders looking in, it appears that the customer vision these companies share never came to realization. In fact, they're still struggling to solve basic business infrastructure issues (structures, people, systems, processes.) To date, we have not seen any data to suggest these acquisition strategies have netted the desired outcomes as far as customers are concerned. If you don't believe it, just look at the numbers.

THE NUMBERS DON'T LIE

The average rate for customer defections is twenty (20%) percent per annum. Taken literally, this means that a company completely recycles its customer base every five years! The reason customers leave are even more disconcerting: a customer feeling ignored or suffering through a bad service experience are issues any company can control. It only gets worse when you look at the numbers more closely. It's amazing how little influence a customer's overall satisfaction has on whether or not the customer leaves. Satisfaction is no longer the appropriate standard for retaining clients. Customers stop doing business with a company even when they are "satisfied" with an experience. Recent surveys of customers who leave organizations conclude that between sixty (60%) percent and seventy (70%) percent of the respondents were either "very satisfied" or "satisfied" with the company and its products and services prior to defecting.[3] What this data strongly suggests is that customers leave even though they may be satisfied with the product, but not with the service or the delivery, or any other thing for that matter. When one "buys" a product/service one really "buys" a company. Just as in our personal life, one doesn't just marry a spouse; one marries a family. It is this revelation that has caused some corporations to focus attention on trying to build customer loyalty.

---

[3] Sewell, Carl and Brown, Paul B. Customers for Life. Simon and Schuster. June, 1998.

As if the minor importance of customer satisfaction isn't disturbing enough, there's the equally startling question of how much an individual customer is worth to a given organization. It may surprise some to learn that there's yet another application of Pareto's Rule: the average company generates eighty (80%) percent of its profits from twenty (20%) percent of its customer base.[4] So individual customers and their respective contributions to the bottom line are not the same! For whatever reason, management tends to dismiss these customer numbers.

I'M OKAY. YOU'RE NOT.

No client has ever hired us because they believed they couldn't keep customers. Even though the concerns that clients confess to us are usually symptomatic of poor customer retention, we get a tremendous amount of resistance from executives over the extent customer defections have on the company and its bottom line. We hear: "There's no way we lose twenty (20%) percent of our clients each year. Our sales goals have increased each year." "We have great customer retention — it's got to be at least ninety-five (95%) percent." Denial... always denial!

Customer defections are viewed as the other guy's problem. Customer retention is a company's "dirty little secret" because strong new sales numbers conceal the true extent of customer losses. This illusion is quickly dispelled when good economic times turn sour. Here's a great illustration:

---

[4] Trepper, Charles. "Customer Care Goes End to End." Information Week. May 15, 2000.

A sales executive from a niche financial services firm asked us to evaluate the service side of the business. He heard some customer complaints (nothing major, mind you) and he viewed our analysis as a preemptive strike. We concluded our assessment and presented our findings to the executive committee. Among the issues we discovered, the company was losing $30 million in assets under management every month. [Annualized this represented about twenty-eight (28%) percent of the firm's total assets under management]. The company president instantly became hostile. He fiercely objected to our statement, even after we showed him his company reports. He quickly changed the objection to "the data is bad." For months, he continued to insist there was no problem with customer defections. The stock market continued to record double digit growth and for the third year in a row, the company's sales increased over thirty (30%) percent. The business was riding high. Then, the technology bubble burst, the stock market tanked and new sales went down...down...down. Only when the lack of new sales stopped masking the assets and customer losses did the president come around.

Then, there are those managers who simply discount customers. A pervasive opinion exists among some corner office residents that customers are replaceable, inter-changeable parts. "We expect to lose a certain percentage of our customers. It's the nature of our business." So long as things don't get too messy (read no lawyers), customer defections are part of doing business. This opinion is most troubling to us because it's so short sighted. How can a business maintain a meaningful relationship with its customers when they're considered passive commodities?

In both cases, some fault is attributable to bad information. Companies don't track customer data or plead ignorance because the information collected on customers is incomplete or unreliable. It is definitely a case of out of sight out of mind. We routinely run into situations with clients where gathering the information necessary to determine the true extent of their customer retention problems is like climbing Mount Everest. Few businesses track revenue and cost details by customer for this data to have real significance. Every business needs to understand the full scope and context of customers who are leaving through the back door.

MANAGEMENT RESPONDS

Under normal circumstances, every senior management team is on a never ending quest for ways to be more cost effective, more productive, and more profitable. Regrettably, customer retention and loyalty are not viewed in these terms, so they are considered backburner issues. They never make it on the executive committee's agenda, unless there's a "crisis."

The more common calamities that put retention on management's radar screen include: a downturn in the business cycle, new sales opportunities slow to a trickle, a large customer leaves (or threatens to do so) or repeated customer defections chip away at the company's renewable revenue. Regardless of the cause, companies respond to customer retention like most business problems—it's a process.

Usually, when a customer threatens to leave, they don't reach that decision overnight. Rather, the customer experiences a series of "dissatisfiers" that leads to the "last straw" and the customer announces his/her intention of leaving. [It's critically important to note that only five (5%) percent of customers announce their intention to leave a firm; most simply walk away without a word].[5] Nonetheless, we'll use the situation where a big customer is threatening to leave a firm as the scenario for our discussion:

STEP 1. Management's initial response is to patch up the immediate troubles — some higher up is immediately dispatched to meet with the customer. The customer's list of grievances is heard. The executive is appalled at what he/she hears, takes copious notes, and makes the appropriate sounds of disgust at exactly the right moment. Upon departing, the manager renews the company's promise of love and devotion and gives the customer assurances that the company will make good. Rest assured the company will do whatever it takes to make things right to prevent these things from happening again, so...

STEP 2. The damage control begins. Management moves swiftly and decisively to fix the corporate malfeasance in question. If, for example, a job or a process is at fault, additional controls are put in place as double or triple checks. If a policy is in question, it's overlooked or fine-tuned or twisted to meet the aggrieved customer's need. With the immediate issues in check...

STEPS 3 AND 4. One can't respond to the long-term until they know who's at fault. It's so much fun seeing this process as it unfolds, with various staff alternatively pointing fingers and ducking for cover. In customer matters, the transgressor is (typically) someone either in the sales or the service organization; although it could be construed as a fatal structural flaw, indicting one of these divisions as a whole. Once blame is determined, senior management

---

[5] Zetocha, Dale. "Retaining Customers by Handling Complaints." North Dakota State University. September, 1996.

convenes a task force or project team to review and recommend changes. Watch out! Let the games begin. The
team/task force holds meeting after meeting where everyone analyzes and argues over the most arcane points. Details of new controls to be devised, new paperwork to be
enacted, new technologies to be initiated are necessary to
produce an exhaustive written report on the matter. There
may also be calls for new responsibilities, new jobs and
even new departments. This group of well meaning zealots
gets so carried away with the work the original mission becomes blurred.

STEP 5. This stage can take one of two tracks. If management determines this is an isolated incident, some of the
project team's solutions are implemented and everybody
gets back to the normal routine until the next crisis. When
the problems are more widespread (or after a series of epi-
sodes), enter the consultants. With recommendations made
and culpability firmly established, now management can
focus its attention on implementing a long-term solution.
The stage is now set for the real heavy lifting. Over the last
decade, senior managers have leaned toward one or another sort of "customer-focused" initiative. The "approach"
taken is based on the determination of the "guilty" culprit
in Step 3. The following table lists some of the common
programs introduced to answer retention/loyalty concerns:

Sales Approach	Service Approach
Customer-focused selling tactics	"Exceptional" service training
Relationship management programs	Improve quality and processes
Frequent-buyer/loyalty programs	Customer performance indicators
Software solutions	Software solutions

Figure 2: Traditional Initiatives to Address Customer Retention and Loyalty Issues

Let's say the committee and consultants conclude that poor data or technology is part of the long-term solution. It's not hard to fathom since, during the 1990s, anything technology related was part of the answer. Businesses turned to Customer Relationship Management (CRM) software, on-line chat customer service, customer tracking databases and other "integrated" systems to improve sales relationships and customer service delivery. Sometimes, these technology solutions are coupled with frequent-buyer programs or other customer loyalty initiatives.

Whatever direction a company takes, the projects guarantee the promise of better, more reliable data, and more cost effective customer processes. If it were only that easy! Gathering ROI figures on any technology project, let alone on projects dealing with customer relationships and service, is an elusive management exercise.[6] Other than quali-

---

[6] The Gardner Group, a technology consulting firm surveyed Fortune 500 CEOs regarding the effectiveness of technology in their organization. As reported in a 1998 Wall Street Journal article, the survey respondents indicated that over forty (40%) percent of the technology

tative measurements of a firm's "customer performance," these programs are hard pressed to deliver tangible bottom line benefits. Suffice it to say there are few documented successes using technology.[7]

Our issue is not with any of the solutions mentioned. There is some value to each of these programs. It's not the committee process. Customer relationships are complex and multi-faceted; neither sales nor customer service has exclusive domain. Any corporate sales, retention or loyalty initiative that attempts to solve the problem through sales or service exclusively will miss the mark. The barriers are institutional. Until management acknowledges and re-solves the systemic nature of these problems, it will remain elusive for companies and their customers to live happily ever after.

---

initiatives instituted in the last three years were not implemented. An-other twenty-eight (28%) percent were scaled back due to cost and schedule overruns. Those surveyed went on to say that even when technology systems were implemented, in seventy-three (73%) percent of the cases the systems did not achieve the efficiencies and benefits originally promised.

[7] Kelley, Joanne. "Jackpot." <u>Content Magazine</u>. September 2001. This article highlights the success of Harrah Entertainment's CRM/customer loyalty project.

CHAPTER 3—WHY NOT HAPPILY EVER AFTER?

Children have never been very good at listening to their elders, but they have never failed to imitate them.

James Baldwin (The Precarious Vogue of Ingmar Bergman, 1960)

I f we change the sales process and monitor customers more effectively, why doesn't retention improve? "Just because..." Those of you who have children know that they ask questions about everything. A simple act like fetching your three-year-old daughter a glass of water at bedtime can produce an astonishing series of rapid-fire questions, each of which reflects her growing frustration with your failure to answer definitively. For instance: "Daddy, why does it rain?" You say, "To make the grass and flowers and trees grow, honey." She says, "How do the clouds know when the trees are thirsty?" You respond with, "The clouds don't know, it just rains." Clearly dissatisfied at this point (or maybe just enjoying the attention), she queries, "Daddy, why don't trees drink from cups?" No doubt really frustrated (and bemused by the unsettling dead-on logic of her inquiries), you give her that patented parental response: "Just because..." (then, you kiss her and turn out the light.)

Just as when a parent, (confronted by a child's continuous abstract or uncomfortable queries) will use the classic way out "...Just because," companies (and their employees), use the same tactic when dealing with customer issues. Corporate "Just because!" allows and sanctions bad behavior and poor decisions within the entire organization. Determine your "Just because!" attitude by answering the following questions:

- Where do customers fit within the organization
- What is the affect of structural and functional alignments on customers
- How do internal power relationships impact customers

Based on our experiences, it appears as if the average company has raised infantile sales and service units, which are ill-equipped to handle the trials and tribulations associated with maintaining healthy, adult-to-adult relationships. When companies use "Just because!" replies they demand that their employees act in a preordained manner. This causes a chain reaction, moving customers in a preordained, time-honored fashion, too: They take their business elsewhere.

We have identified three corporate "Just because!" scenarios gleaned from our consulting experiences. Two of the three we have observed first hand in every single company with whom we have been associated. While the third response is less prevalent (we've seen this problem with half of our clients), it is the hardest to overcome and the most debilitating to the company and to customer relationships. That's where we shall begin, just because...

WHO IS YOUR CUSTOMER?

The first questions we ask senior executives when we interview them are: "Who is your customer?" and "Tell us why?" Imagine the embarrassment when we tell the executive team that there were conflicting answers to these fundamental questions! CEOs just reach for the Alka Seltzer. Case in point:

We worked with a very successful insurance company whose core business was to provide retirement annuities to employees working in the not-for-profit world. Since their inception, this company believed that their customer was the independent insurance agent who sold their products. While the company had extensive structures to support policyholders, the vast majority of its infrastructure was designed to meet the needs of the insurance reps. It had a stellar reputation among agents and the company prospered for decades with great new sales and high asset/client retention.

Then another, larger insurance company acquired the firm. They also had a strong presence in the retirement marketplace and used the same distribution channel. Once the dust from the acquisition settled, a new CEO was appointed. He came up through the ranks of the parent company. It wasn't long before he declared that the policyholder was now the company's customer. Just because! Over the next several years, this reassessment turned the company's infrastructure on its head. Its systems, policies and practices had to be retooled to support the policyholder. It didn't take long for agents to notice the difference and they took their business (and their clients) elsewhere. It took less than three years for the company to go from an industry leader to an "also ran." After a couple more years of lower sales and millions in lost assets, the company quietly reestablished the agent as the customer. Unfortunately, it was a case of "too little, too late"; the damage was already done. The firm could not regain the trust (or the business) of the independent agents. The story doesn't end there.

In an even more ironic twist, a global financial services firm then acquired the parent company. The global organization also had a large, successful business unit in the same marketplace, but their customer was neither the independent agent nor the policyholder; it was the employer. Imagine the confusion that resulted over whom to sell and service. Two years after the last merger, the business units in this marketplace are still reconciling their customer differences.

This is obviously an extreme example. At first, we thought it was an anomaly within the financial services industry but as our work expanded into other industries, our premise proved untrue. Here's what we now know.

Companies with direct retail channels usually know their customer. When an issue arises, it's usually around customer segmentation (we'll save this topic for discussion later.) B-to-B companies, businesses with independent sales distribution channels and those with both retail and wholesale outlets, are more likely to have disagreements over who is the customer. Here are examples of the troubles we have seen:

- Identifying the wrong customer (we've really seen it)
- Trying to support more than one client constituency with the same sales and service structure, attempting to be "everything to everybody"
- Mistaking a strategic partner for the customer

In the last example, firms have a "strategic partner "

44

they believe gives them a competitive advantage by granting them exclusive access to a particular customer base (even though these customers are also accessible to competitors through normal sales distribution channels.) Nonetheless, these businesses serviced the "access grantors" and not the real customers to whom they sold their services and generated their revenue. These businesses had customer retention problems that went well beyond the norm.

When we run into inconsistencies over "Who is the customer?" more often than not it is a form of corporate schizophrenia. The firm attempts to serve more than one master with the same infrastructure. Having more than one distribution channel or multiple customer constituencies is not necessarily a problem in itself. Going back to our earlier example, all three of the companies were successful in the same market even though they each focused on a different customer population within that marketplace. Their success was based on aligning the organization's infrastructure to sell and service one particular customer.

Obviously, when a business cannot verbalize clearly the identity of the customer and delivers "just because" answers, any attempt at a genuine customer relationship immediately sours. It also tells us that extensive infrastructure repair and coaching are needed to get the relationships on track. However, don't get lulled into a false sense of security if your company does not suffer from this dilemma. The next several "Just because!" conditions are universal, regardless of industry or distribution channels. They have equally devastating effects on customer relationships.

WE'VE ALWAYS DONE THINGS THIS WAY

Where does the customer fit in the organization? Most employees interpret how to answer this question by what senior management does, not what it says. Employees hear corporate leaders give politically correct answers like, "We value our customers," or "The customer is always right." But, how do they really act? Here's what one consulting client did before they retained our services:

A grand program was announced at their national sales conference. The goal was for employees to focus more attention on customer retention. The company president outlined his expectations, unveiled a catchy slogan and showed off the cool promotional items designed to tout the company's commitment to its customers and to the initiative. By management's own admission, these actions were warranted because getting the sales force to concentrate on retention was a major change for the company. On the surface, the company played the right strategy.

Six months later management was actually surprised to learn that its retention rate actually got worse. What we learned (through a bit of digging) was that management unintentionally gave the staff lots of non-verbal, "We've always done things this way" messages. First, senior management never considered changing the reward system that paid employees exclusively on making sales to new customers. Nor did they give a second thought to the sales contest initiated to bring in new customers a few months after the conference. Even though they spoke about the importance of current customers they never thought about implementing any changes to reach out to them in the service units—the people who interacted with current customers the most. In hindsight, it was easy for the leadership to see how they negatively influenced the outcome of their initiative given all the mixed messages they sent.

The "We've always done things this way" messages from senior management take on many forms. Since the days of the Industrial Revolution, entrepreneurs and academics have handed down an array of hierarchical schemes and functional configurations in order to better organize and align resources. Whether a business structure is flat or designed like a pyramid, organized by product or geography, resources are always clustered by business discipline. Likewise, authority is bestowed along functional lines for the planning, decision making and problem solving by expertise. People problems...hand them off to Human Resources. Computer woes...IT does that stuff. What about customer concerns? Well, first you need to be more specific. If it's a pre-sale quagmire, then ship it off to sales. A post-sale issue, funnel it to customer service. Specialization is what management knows. Why? "Just because!"

For the record, we agree that some business specialization is essential; in fact, it's an absolute necessity in some professional disciplines. For example, specialization ensures that proper controls are maintained. We would be the first ones to yell "foul" if we saw an internal auditor issuing accounts payable checks. Specialization also acknowledges certain expertise. Clearly, a patent attorney is not well suited to perform corporate tax work.

In most organizations, sales and service responsibilities are considered distinct customer deliverables, even though they have joint responsibility for the customer relationship. Since both groups have customer responsibilities, it seems logical that sales and service would actively coordinate activities. Do your sales and service organizations conduct joint business planning? Chances are they don't! Instead, they slice and dice customer relationships based on established sales and service structures, job responsibilities and decision making authority.

One of our clients launched a new investment product and, from the moment it was introduced to the sales force it practically sold itself. After a couple weeks of record breaking sales, however, problems began to plague other areas of the company. Customers (also in record numbers) were calling sales people to complain about lost paperwork, processing delays, incorrect information, and bad attitudes. The sales force started screaming that the customer service and operational units (the service organization) were screwing things up big time. That's when we got the call.

After a bit of digging, it turned out the service organization was "screwing up" because the company's existing information processing system could not support the new product. IT was still working on the necessary system upgrades but they were still months away from testing. The manual workflow processes were being implemented on the fly. Customer service performance problems stemmed from the fact they didn't have specific information about the new product (let alone training) to answer customer questions. Then we discovered that the service organization learned of the product launch when the paperwork started coming in the door.

This example may seem extreme but trust us; it's not. We regularly run into situations where the service organization, encased in its own structure, has no idea what the sales side of the business is doing. On the surface, it seems logical to bring sales and service together to solve these work coordination problems, but for some reason, management doesn't make this leap.

Many companies realize there are huge benefits to attacking certain business issues across departmental boundaries. On one hand, it's very easy to find examples where a multi-disciplinary approach was successful for "special projects." Most of us, usually working as middle managers, have participated in many successful initiatives working in a cross-functional team. But, when strategic issues are handled in a multi-disciplinary fashion, the efforts fail. Results tend to be measured more by pointing fingers and winning turf wars. If the group is fortunate, they may agree on the wording of some grandiose statement about the company's strategic direction. These "what we're going to do" declarations rarely lead to actions, let alone real change.

Sales and service specialization impedes companies from building long-term, profitable customer relationships. When the left hand (service) doesn't know what the right hand (sales) has promised, is it any wonder why so many customers become discontent and take their business elsewhere. Even when customers do stay, the self-imposed wall between sales and service does nothing to promote additional sales or cross-selling opportunities.

An organization's tendency to segregate business activities and decision making does not tell the whole story alone. The traditional bastions of corporate power work hand in hand with the organization's formal lines of specialization to cause the final "just because" trend.

SIBLING RIVALRIES

There's a pecking order in every relationship, every family and every business. It's irrelevant whether these rankings are real or perceived because the perception alone makes it a reality. Someone always wears the pants (in the family); the oldest sibling believes in the destiny of their natural birthright; and, companies sort things out relative to P&L impact. Sales and service are polar extremes. Sales is in the plus column, a revenue generator. Sales and marketing expense is simply a cost of doing business. The service organization (i.e. operations, IT and customer service), in turn, operates as a "cost center." This dichotomy between sales and service has other far-reaching effects.

Sales and service people are wired differently: different skill sets, competing interests and egos that make it difficult to deliver on customers' needs in a singular fashion. Sales and service divisions tend to work at cross-purposes. Similar to those Republicans and Democrats in the U.S. Congress who give lip service about working in a "bipartisan spirit" (and yet work behind the scenes to undermine the other), the open contempt between the two professions is palpable. A while back we developed a keynote presentation version of *CellMates to SoulMates*. The following table illustrates in a humorous way the personal undercurrents that exist between the two groups.

Sales Skill	"Service Says...They're"	Service Skill	"Sales Says...They're"
Assertive	*Pushy*	Problem-solver	*Excuse-maker*
Verbal	*Empty suits*	Supportive	*Manic*
Resilient	*Pompous*	Caring	*Wishy-washy*
Customer-focused	*Promise anything*	Customer-focused	*Bureaucrat*

Figure 3: "Sales Says, Service Says"

These adjectives are an accurate portrayal of how sales and service people really view one another. The comments come from real people. We suggest the organizational dynamics — namely the corporate prejudice swirling around the two units is the root cause of the unhealthy rivalry. Sales (having the advantage of a preordained station top in corporate life) is in the driver's seat, exerting power, influence and control. Service sits uncomfortably in the back seat, staring at the landscape passing them by, daydreaming, "If only things were different..." We should not be surprised by these attitudes because they are only products of their environment.

Like some precocious child prodigies, from a very early age Sales sees and hears how special they are. Sales has a special pay and incentive system. Sales gets all the operating and capital money they need at budget time — even money for all those promotional trinkets. No wonder it's common for sales people to quip, "We pay your salary!"

Charles Perrault's classic fairy tale Cinderella provides a perfect type-cast for the service organization. Service, cast as Cinderella, plays the convincing stepdaughter. Close your eyes and imagine. Hear the stepmother clearly articulate the rules of the game: "Service. You're insignificant, a cost of doing business." Service responds as directed, never venturing outside, tirelessly toiling away in cubicles, sitting by the phone, waiting, hoping for a chance. If only the prince would call. "Just because!"

We were performing an assignment in a client's service department. While interviewing an operational processor, a sales representative approached with paperwork for a new customer. The salesperson expressed excitement in having "landed" this particular customer and made clear that it was essential that these documents be handled immediately. The processor assured the salesperson that he would comply. The salesperson left happily, unaware that the processor slipped the paperwork to the bottom of a huge mound of work complaining as he did about how overworked he was and that he didn't have time to handle this special request. How's that for passive aggressive behavior!

How can you have healthy, long-term relationships with your customers when those responsible for the relationships don't work together? The natural disconnections we see in the sales process coupled with the systemic corporate barriers require a fundamental rethinking of the relationship between sales and service. Sales and service must become one.

CHAPTER 4—"I DO"

"Whatever I have tried to do in life, I have tried with my heart to do well."

Charles Dickens

"To have and to hold from this day forward, for better for worse, for richer, for poorer, in sickness and in health, to love and to cherish, till death us do part..."[8] "I do" is the culmination of a life altering personal commitment full of expectations and dreams. The "vows" made between a company and customer are also crammed with hopes and aspirations. When two parties freely and knowingly make promises, no one has expectations the union will ever end.

We just compared the relationship between a company and its customers to the relationship created by marriage. We realize this analogy may set a dangerous precedent. [On the advice of counsel, note to our spouses: any statements or references to relationships with respect to marriage contained herein are not based on personal experience].

Some cynic out there will no doubt remember the statistics on customer retention we quoted earlier and conclude that businesses do a better job at keeping customers than

---

[8] Kueppers, Sandra (Editor). <u>Book of Common Prayer Wedding Service</u>. 1945.

men and women do at staying out of divorce court. The skeptic says, "The average company loses twenty (20%) percent of its customers and fifty (50%) percent of all marriages end in divorce." In fact, the twenty (20%) percent of customers who defect is an annual number. If customer retention and divorce figures were comparable, no one would ever give Liz Taylor's marriage chronicles a second thought.

Remember the basic premise of our argument for change—a company can't have healthy relationships with its customers if those responsible for that union (sales and service) are themselves unhealthy and conflicted. The company must right itself internally before it can deliver on customer commitments. Getting the sales and service units to work in concert is the only thing truly under management's control. Customers and their behaviors are not. By establishing positive internal relationships organizations can commit entirely to their customers, and in turn, determine what is realistically needed to support those external relationships.

WHY SAY "I DO"

By now you may be saying that this process can't happen in your organization, "There is too much water under the bridge; this might work with a start-up business that is not weighed down with history. We are too set in our ways, too entrenched in bureaucracy, and there are too many preconceived notions about sales and service." While we have supported several start-up operations that wanted to integrate sales and service from day one, our typical client normally operates in mature industries and has been in business for ten or more years. Before we get the initial call an organization frequently has endured flat or decreasing revenues, inefficient work processes, and a poor customer service reputation. These warning signs are commonly coupled with unsuccessful attempts by senior management to right the perceived wrongs.

Our clients are not on life support. The sales and service model is not designed to help an organization that cannot sustain itself in the near term. When a company is one step away from bankruptcy; they don't need consultants to initiate or sanction the drastic cost-reduction tactics necessary to survive. The model does not mesh with corporations operating on a short-term horizon either. If the firm is searching for a quick fix to boost quarterly earnings, it is best to look elsewhere. Once a company implements our model, it takes three to six months before it sees measurable bottom line benefits and twelve to eighteen months to see more dramatic results. Now that we've identified the type of companies ready to say, "I do" it's important to discuss the key values of integration and the organizational conversion they necessitate.

THE IDEALS OF "I DO"

When an organization says, "I do" to integrating sales and service, it commits to three tenets, which collectively embody a significant paradigm shift for employees and the business as a whole.

- Sales and service is part of the same continuous process
- Sales and service is everything the company does
- Sales and service is everybody's job

What do these principles mean to you and your employees? If you accept this new way to do business, what changes can you expect to see? Here's an overview of each tenet and what it signifies to an organization.

THE SALES AND SERVICE PROCESS—IT'S THE SAME

Integration begins with a fresh understanding of the traditional sales process itself. We must stop viewing the sales process as linear and separate from the rest of the customer relationship. Stop thinking that there are pre-sale and post-sale components. That conventional wisdom is flawed. The new, integrated "sales and service" process is an uninterrupted circle. It's as "easy" as A, B, C:

Acquire new customers

Build customer loyalty and

Cultivate additional sales opportunities from those customers

**CULTIVATE
ADDITIONAL SALES**

A brief explanation of the A, B, Cs will give you a clearer understanding of the concepts surrounding our sales and service model.

"A" ACQUIRE NEW CUSTOMERS

This is a collaborative effort on the part of both sales and service to turn prospects into paying customers. To achieve this objective, we introduce "smarter" sales strategies and tactics while simultaneously reworking the service organization so it can properly support both the sales division and customers.

Service must provide sales with realistic information regarding its capabilities to deliver on customer needs. When the sales force is equipped with the specifics about what it takes to get products or services delivered, they can manage customer expectations and meet customer needs with certainty time and again.

Service must make experts readily available to answer customer questions (and objections) regarding the execution and delivery of the product. Firms that sell expensive, more complex products must bring technical experts into the process, as a prospect gets more serious. It's a tool that can be used cost effectively in almost any selling environment.

Sales must do a better job identifying the right customers for the business. It's a matter of quelling sale's "desire" to sell anything to anyone and replace it with an understanding of the prospective customer's longevity and profitability on the business.

Once the deal is closed, it is the duty of both groups to become accountable to the customer ensuring that his/her needs are met. This is where better communication and co-ordination of work enters into the picture, which leads us to the next phase of the sales and service process.

"B" BUILD CUSTOMER LOYALTY

> A business builds loyalty by performing its customer responsibilities in a manner that reinforces a customer's original purchase decision.

Building customer loyalty commences Day One when sales creates a sincere and respectful relationship with a prospective client. Loyalty germinates when sales sets realistic expectations which are met by the service organization. Loyalty is further perpetuated through the use of proactive sales/service tactics that are intended to keep the customer connected to the organization. For example, make periodic, personal contact with customers—touching base to see that the customer was satisfied, following up on service requests or purchase orders, getting feedback on a new product development idea. They are all ways to keep the customer engaged.

Interestingly, our dentists offer a great illustration about building customer loyalty. Every patient expects to receive post treatment instructions from their dentist. If you have soreness, rinse with warm salt water. If you have pain, take a pain-reliever. If you have bleeding, call the office. Our dentists do this as standard procedure, but since it's a normal expectation for a patient, it (in itself) does nothing to build loyalty. Our dentists go one step further. At the end of every business day, they personally call every patient seen in the office that day. It doesn't matter whether they came in for a cleaning or an impacted tooth extraction— they call each patient. "How are you feeling?" "Are you experiencing any problems?" "Do you have any pain?"

They end the call by saying, "don't hesitate to call me" if you have any questions or problems. This simple act not only shows a genuine concern for their patient's welfare, but it translates into greater loyalty. Customer loyalty is essential to move a customer to the next stage of the process.

"C" CULTIVATE ADDITIONAL SALES OPPORTUNITIES

"Cultivate additional sales opportunities" takes into consideration all the different means to resell customers. It's what we refer to as the "3 Rs": repeat, recurring and referral sales. Once (and only once) the organization that has created this sense of loyalty, it is in the position to take advantage of the 3 Rs.

A few years back a client was lamenting that even though they regularly sent newsletters and promotional material to existing customers, they rarely generated customer calls let alone additional sales. We asked what else they did to sustain customer relationships. There was silence. The moral:

> Far too many companies hold the mistaken belief that reselling customers is an inalienable right attained simply because a customer made an initial purchase.

Firms arrive at this conclusion based on two assumptions. First, the product or service is delivered as promised. Second, the product or service is performing as promised. As a consequence, firms conduct extensive marketing campaigns with existing customers to generate repeat sales. Even when these conditions are true (and how would one know since most businesses don't track them), sending expensive marketing materials, product catalogs or e-mail promotions is an exercise in futility. As we previously illustrated, meeting basic customer expectations does nothing for the company other than enabling them to stay in the game.

> Reselling customers is a *privilege* that businesses win through extraordinary actions.

Expanding on our earlier example, both of us have referred friends and family members to our dentists. What causes someone to make a referral? First and foremost, one's basic expectations are met. The services our dentists provide are excellent. It goes without saying that if they did shoddy work we would find another dentist ourselves. It's also true that if they just did excellent work, there wouldn't be any reason to recommend them—there are lots of first-rate dentists. We're motivated to make the referral because we're confident our dentists will treat our loved ones with the same extraordinary care and concern we receive. In the final analysis, the campaigns to build loyalty and cultivate the 3 Rs go hand in hand.

SALES AND SERVICE IS EVERYTHING THE COMPANY DOES

In an integrated company, both functions—the sales organization and the service organization—support all aspects of the customer relationship. Integrating sales and service is more than better methods and improved coordination of work; it's a business strategy. Businesses use mission and vision statements in an attempt to paint a clear picture for employees and other stakeholders about its purpose in life. Academics apply characterizations like "sales driven" or "research driven" in an attempt to describe the company's center of influence. In our integration model, the center of influence is the customer. It takes a more pragmatic view of the organization with respect to its mission in life. The business must look at itself differently. By making sales and service one, the organization can focus on the customer.

Research and development, marketing, sales (of course) and similarly situated groups remain part of a traditional sales structure. In addition to working smarter (read customer profitability), they remain engaged in customer relationships after the initial sale is made. The rest of the organization is free to focus on service. Whether or not an individual department has direct customer contact— everything supports the execution and delivery of products and services to customers. When one accepts this view of a sales and service organization, perspectives change:

- Sales manages customer relationships over the long-term seeking opportunities to generate repeat, recurring and referrals sales
- Customer billing becomes something more than an accounting function; the design, use and accuracy of a customer invoice impacts customer relationships
- Information Technology builds systems to support customer needs
- Operational units become the prime "deliverers" of the company's products and services processes

The final tenet is a natural extension of the first two.

SALES AND SERVICE IS EVERYBODY'S JOB

When the sales and service process is perpetual and sales and service becomes everything the organization does, the everyday work people do is also transformed. The old division of labor (and the roles it defined) no longer applies. Everyone in the company is a salesperson; everyone is a service provider. This requires employees to alter mindsets, learn new skills, and modify behaviors, which are the real nuts and bolts of any organizational change.

First, the business must create an environment that encourages this new mindset. A company must recognize that it needs loyal employees to build long-term relationships with customers. Building customer loyalty takes time and effort and the constant turnover of employees insures that somebody is always low on the learning curve and cannot provide meaningful support. Short-term employees cannot build long-term relationships. To align employees behind sales and service implementation, the company must deal with staff as adults:

- Create a clear customer vision that employees rally behind
- Communicate the good, the bad and the ugly honestly to build trust and respect within the company
- Handle issues that affect employee work and their livelihood with care and diligence

Don't ignore the notion of treating employees as adults. Unless employees buy-in and become engaged in the integration process, it will not be successful over the long-term. Integration works best when senior management leads by example providing employees with a model for building loyal customers by building trust and respect among employees. Show them the company means what it says, when it says, "We treat customers the way we want to be treated."

With a better understanding of the principles behind sales and service integration, we can focus on the specific ways to make it a reality. Corporate relationships, just as in personal relationships, work best when the partners:

- Want the same things...
- Communicate...
- Work at it...

The remaining chapters show you how to do it.

CHAPTER 5—WANTING THE SAME THINGS

"To place before mankind the common sense of the subject — in terms so plain and firm as to command their assent."

Thomas Jefferson

General likes and dislikes dictate whether two people will decide to date. Is there some basic attraction (eyes, hair, car, money, brains, sense of humor, butt, brawn?) When there's no match, the process ends. If, however, the initial impressions of the two people are favorable, with each passing date, the assessments become more and more profound. What things do we really have in common (class, camping, food, therapists, sports, romantic walks?) As things get more serious, so do the questions (dreams, ambitions, career goals, potential in-laws, sexual performance, furniture motifs, children, pets.) We ask these questions to see whether we're compatible. Do we want the same things? It is from this step-by-step evaluation that a critical mass is formulated and molded into a shared life plan. Just as in personal interactions, sales and service must be compatible. To create an integrated strategic plan (i.e. a life plan), sales and service must want the same things. It starts with a unifying vision.

THE CUSTOMER VISION

Every manager has read some book, heard some B-school professor, or listened to the grand proclamation of some consultant pontificating about the need for a mission or vision statement to focus the organization on a particular goal. We presume some time in your business career you worked with a group in an attempt to write a corporate message full of platitudes and idealisms, or you helped create a promotional slogan, that was then dutifully printed on banners, mugs, or other corporate "memorabilia." That's not what we're implying or want for this vision statement. We don't promote or condone all that "pie in the sky" fluff.

However, a well-constructed customer vision statement is both a powerful motivational tool and a decision barometer. The aim is to paint a verbal picture of the future in clear and concise terms (thank you Thomas Jefferson.) Change management research clearly shows a strong correlation between vision statements, planning and goal-setting in leading to successful projects.[9] For employees, the customer vision provides direction, a touchstone that promotes the "end game." From a motivational standpoint, it creates anticipation and energy that can be converted into employee approval and buy-in. In other words, a customer vision becomes the rallying cry for the workforce—unifying the company to reach the desired goals.

Vision statements can also direct senior management's actions and decision making through the course of the project. As the integration process unfolds, all sorts of issues

[9] Davis, Brian L., Skube, Carol J., Hellervik, Lowell W., Gelbelein, Susan H., and Sheard, James L. Successful Manager's Handbook: *Development Suggestions for Today's Managers*. Personnel Decisions, Inc. 1992.

come to the attention of the senior team. By weighing those matters against the vision, they can be placed in proper perspective, prioritized and acted upon accordingly.

As you draft a vision statement, avoid the grandiose, public relations approach. Summarize the organization's desire for profitable and loyal customers in a declaration that is impossible to misunderstand and hard to forget. The best statements are real and to the point. Once the vision is in place, we can concentrate on more tangible outcomes.

SHARED CUSTOMER GOALS

Similarly, you recognize that creating shared goals for sales and service must be performed in the broader context of the organization's strategic and business planning. Since integration must overlay those plans, instead of providing a typical blueprint for strategic and business planning, we are going to focus only on those matters related to integration that must be addressed during any goal-setting discussions.

Reaching agreement on shared goals requires senior executive collaboration and cooperation. The collective health of the senior team along with personal issues around competition, trust and respect will greatly influence the process. However, remember this is an arranged marriage. While the company president cannot legislate respect, he/she can influence the betrothed parties to cooperate and give integration a chance.

The process must begin with what we call the "customer fit." Start the goal-setting discussions answering the following questions:

- Based on corporate history, what types of customers (demographically speaking) are best suited for the organization?

- Which current (or past) customers can be looked to as ideals in terms of loyalty? In terms of profitability?
- Conversely, what current customers should be used as models *to avoid* going forward?
- In both cases, what are the *specific* characteristics that make those customers models?

After the team has identified the good and bad prototypes, we recommend that the executives candidly discuss the history of those customers with the company. These historical discussions are critical to the process as they reveal specific (and many times controllable) events or actions that led customers down a particular path. Under no circumstances should the group allow this session to become filled with name calling and finger pointing. Once the group reaches consensus on the answers to these questions, they can drill down to the next level of detail.

SWAPPING BIAS FOR BALANCE

In earlier chapters we discussed how and why customers go away. Our observations have centered on the destructive behaviors of sales and service people as well as the routine ways organizations enable those actions to occur as a customer progresses through the pre-sale and post-sale stages. Some may notice the underlying theme peppered throughout our arguments:

> There is an unconscious caste system between new and existing customers in most companies. The disparity exists over the perceived value of new customers versus customers already sold.

If management does not address this disparity in goal-setting, we guarantee that inequity will forever rear its ugly head. The business will continue to see its customer base erode and literally destroy the company's chance to integrate sales and service. The primary concern to creating shared goals is to establish balance:

> Goals must reflect realistic objectives for <u>both</u> new customers and existing customers.

An existing customer's worth (as an investment) is undeniable: when cultivated actively, they are always more profitable. Determining a customer's long-term value (profitability) is the subject of many books and articles and we're sure you've heard statistics like, "...acquiring a new customer takes 4 to 6 times more effort than reselling an existing one...."[10] So, we are not going to bore you by re-

---

[10] Statistics comparing the cost of selling new customer versus the cost of selling existing customer vary widely. The conventional wisdom is that it is significantly cheaper to sell to existing customers, however, finding a valid study and a consensus number about how much

hashing the same old details[11] about this subject. Instead, we want you to consider these interrelated issues as you set goals:

- How should new and existing customers "fit" into the company's overall growth plans
- What are realistic sales and service objectives for generating new, repeat, recurring and referral sales
- What is an optimal profit margin for new versus current customers
- What customer retention rate do we need to achieve and over what time period
- How should the business measure customer loyalty

In addition, the executive team needs to work though a series of goals related to the nuts and bolts of integrating sales and service—from streamlining processes and coordinating work efforts to performing tasks that perpetuate the 3 Rs. [As a result, we advise you to incorporate these objectives after finishing the book and revisit baseline integration goals at three and six months after launch to ensure they remain relevant to initiative].

---

cheaper has been elusive. Over the years we have seen or heard various figures indicating that selling current customers is 2, 4, 5 to as much as 10 times less expensive than selling new ones. Our own client experiences also confirm reselling to existing customers is less expensive.

[11] For further information on the subject we suggest paging through Frederick F. Reichheld's book The Loyalty Effect. It provides a sophisticated financial framework on both customer value and profitability. You can also visit to our website www.cbsg.com and go to our Request Information page. In the subject, type "CellMates Profit Material" and will e-mail additional material and worksheets.

COMPENSATION AND REWARD SYSTEMS

No corporate initiative is taken seriously unless there are measurable goals and rewards. The goal-setting discussions require a reevaluation of the organization's compensation and reward structures. Existing pay programs perpetuate the problems that the firm is trying to solve through integration. Therefore, maintaining the status quo with respect to compensation and rewards will ensure that sales and service integration will never be more than a twinkle in the CEO's eye. Prior to integration, our clients have fallen into one of two compensation traps:

- *Compensation Trap 1:* Sales compensation is front-loaded to reward new customer sales revenue with just token incentives for generating the 3 Rs (repeat, recurring or referral sales); while, incentive pay for the service organization is ignored completely
- *Compensation Trap 2:* Sales compensation is back-loaded to reward recurring sales revenue with nominal incentives for generating new customer sales; again, the service organization is ignored

Both of these compensation structures exclusively focus on the sales side of the business. What's interesting is that both schemes produce predicable results. Companies get exactly that for which they paid.

Trap 1 firms are hyper sales driven businesses, frantically moving from relationship to relationship, searching for the next new sale. When things are humming, they have lots of new customers and great sales figures. However, sales from the "3R" sources are indiscernible (and never measured.) As one might expect, customer defection rates are well above average—bordering on the horrendous. The service side of the business is just as frenzied churning out work in order to keep pace.

Trap 2 companies are prodding and methodical, except for the occasional fire drill. They enjoy a predicable cash flow from repeat or recurring sales (referral sales are infrequent). On the other hand, these firms tend to experience flat or slow sales growth, since acquiring new customers is not a sales priority. Customer retention tends to be average. There's an interesting twist at work with these firms. When a customer defects, a new customer magically appears who just happens to generate a remarkably similar revenue stream. Imagine that. [It's amazing what sales people can accomplish once they have established a certain standard of living]. The service side tends to be more methodical, bordering on the bureaucratic. Rules and procedures are put in place to regulate customer work.

Neither trap pays to incent the service side of the business. While it is not uncommon to find a bonus program in place for these folks, such plans are usually "productivity-based." Service is rewarded for how much "stuff" they do, but not the things that cultivate additional sales. Regardless of the compensation trap a company employs, an organization ends up in the same place. There are not enough customers generating enough profitable business to sustain the company over the long-term or during economic downturns.

Devising healthy compensation and incentive plans that substantiate parity will vary from business to business and from industry to industry; so some of our ideas work successfully for your particular business, while others are less appropriate. The compensation and reward structures need to work hand in glove with the firm's shared goals:

> Pay systems should be balanced, rewarding new
> sales and 3R sales similarly.

Both sales and service employees should be paid and rewarded accordingly. Likewise, the program must promote cooperation and collaboration between sales and service. In other words, the incentive structure should place less emphasis on the individual and more on group contributions. Finally, companies need to establish a reasonable ratio between the lowest and highest paid employees.

The above comments call for you to once again suspend your disbelief. We recognize that they fly in the face of customary pay practices. To some, downplaying individual performance and risk/reward models may appear almost anti-capitalist. We did not reach these opinions hastily. They are based on witnessing too many exclusive and excessive pay packages.

To evaluate your company's compensation and incentive programs ask yourself the following questions. An answer of "True" to three or more of the queries signifies an organization with disproportionate pay practices:

- Are more than twenty-five (25%) percent of total sales incentive and/or compensation paid as an exception to the standard rates
- Are there "special" incentive deals paid to certain executives, sales professionals or other favored sons or daughters
- Is more than fifty (50%) percent of the company's workforce either ineligible for or does not meet the

required standards to get an incentive
- Do management personnel receive fifty (50%) percent or more of the company's total bonus pool
- Is the ratio between your lowest and highest paid (total compensation) employees greater than 100 to 1[12]

Obviously, every company has a limited amount of money to pay for salaries and incentives. These dollars must balance individual and team performance, labor market conditions, the element of risk/reward and corporate profitability. Here are a few suggestions we have used to reward people based on these ideologies:

- Eliminate exclusive use of front or back-loaded sales compensation. If, for example, your company pays a different commission rate for new customer sales versus existing customer sales, then close that gap to make it worthwhile for the sales folks to pursue both avenues.
- Stop paying sales commissions and/or incentives on unprofitable transactions. Establish minimum sale levels on which commissions will be paid that reflect the costs associated with selling/servicing customers.

---

[12] We arrived at this idea of paying CEOs no more than 100 times the lowest paid employee based on the results of several 2001 executive compensation surveys including those conducted by: Hewitt Associates, Business Week and the Wall Street Journal/Mercer Human Resource Consulting. Among the findings: in 1982 the average CEO pay was 42 times greater than the lowest paid worker. In 2001, surveys quoted CEO pay numbers that were between 400 and 500 times higher than the lowest paid worker.

- Provide incentive compensation to those on the service side that make and facilitate sales. Also apportion a percent of all sales[13] to the service side of the business.
- Run a contest to promote sales to the customers who have been neglected in the past. This is a great way to get the sales and service people to refocus on those opportunities.
- Don't allow your incentive plans to be viewed as "entitlements." Having a minimum benchmark that changes annually will help to ensure that doesn't happen. Just be sure the goals are challenging yet achievable. If the goals are too easy, it breeds entitlement. When the goals are unrealistic they become irrelevant.
- Reign in the excesses. The only thing the extravagant pay and self-indulgent perks motivate is resentment.[14]
- Keep things as simple as possible. Focus attention on a few key measurements that people can understand, relate to and impact.

---

[13] At one time we advocated some form of profit sharing throughout the company to get employees to pay attention to the bottom line. Over time, we modified this position for everyone except senior executives because there are simply too many profit variables outside of the control of most employees.

[14] William J. McDonough, President of the Federal Reserve of New York, spoke on the excessive executive compensation during his highly publicized speech on September 11, 2002. He called the run-up in CEO compensation "terribly bad social policy and perhaps even bad morals."

As you contemplate how to restructure your compensation and incentives, remember that you must share the financials with the entire organization. It is commonplace for privately held companies not to share financial results with its employees. [It may come as a surprise to some but it's common for even senior executives of these firms to be in the dark about the financials]. If a company expects to install a viable incentive program, the financials must be communicated to employees. If employees are asked to help reduce expenses, they need to see the company's current financial condition as well as the fruits of their efforts. This practice is not easy for private owners to swallow, but speaking from experience, those companies that share financial data with employees (versus those that do not) experienced significantly better financial results through our program. The financial transparency led to more trust and buy-in.

For those of you that have intimate knowledge of the parties involved in this undertaking, you're thinking, oh boy, how are we going to get sales and service to want the same things?

THE POLITICS OF INTEGRATION

We cannot end this discussion without addressing organizational change and politics. Here comes the old cliché about needing executive buy-in to make this thing work.

It's much easier to implement when the executive team is leading and championing integration from the outset. Eventually a true coalition (an influential plurality) of senior team members must buy into the program for the initiative to take root. However, it is not a prerequisite to begin. All you need is one leader to get things started...

Obviously, when the President/CEO backs integration from the beginning, executive support is not an issue. If not the CEO, an enlightened Chief Sales Officer or Chief Operating Officer will do just fine with one caveat: the executive champion must have major influence both with the President and within the organization. Regardless of the individual's job title, take comfort in the fact that, with few exceptions, we began every integration initiative with a lone senior manager supporting the cause. [For the record, more often than not it was the sales executive leading the way]. For those not sitting in a corner office, don't dismay. We also worked through middle management building support up the corporate ladder to launch an integration initiative.

No matter where in management one resides, it is a fairy tale to think that you'll get the entire senior management group to back the initiative from the beginning (even if the CEO is in your corner from the outset). Expect resistance. In the best of circumstances, we don't remember ever launching an integration process without some executive resistance.

Be alert and work hard to build consensus. Identify where that executive resistance exists and discover the individual "hot buttons" of those who have the power to influence others. The biggest mistake one can make is to avoid powerful resistors and their issues with the program (regardless of the validity of the issues.) Embrace their concerns, address their "issues" head on, and (more often than not) you can get enough of them on to your side to form a coalition. We have a couple additional words of caution about resistance:

- Don't get discouraged; the resistance at the senior level passes relatively quickly; but—
- Even when you have a coalition that supports the initiative, never ever be lulled into a false sense of

security; because —

The greatest, most persistent source of resistance will come from the ranks of middle management.

DEALING WITH MIDDLE CHILDREN

We hate to generalize but middle management, as a group, is terrified of change. They are so afraid of losing control of their domains or getting involved in anything they think could risk their security or status in the company. As a rule, most middle managers dig in and subversively work to prevent change. Imagine a corporation as an extended family. Middle managers are the middle child. They feel squeezed between the spoiled, aggressive oldest child and the precocious, indulged youngest. They feel unloved, unheard and lost in the family hierarchy. They believe the only way they can survive is to stubbornly hold on to what little they have been given.

An informal communal system is at play in all companies — a loose network of smaller family units that make up the broader clan. These smaller units offer their members love and support day after day and loyalty within these groups is stronger than the loyalty to the "family" as a whole. Each of these sub-units has their own leaders and "standards." As we relate these leaders and the rules back to organizational life, we have a bunch of middle children influencing the pace of work, and more notably, the entire sub-group's feelings toward and its relationship to upper management. When the broader organization and its leaders accept a proposed change, events will proceed more smoothly assuming enough of the leaders of these small family units are aboard with the change. If too many are opposed (and/or they are ignored or feel ignored), change can be derailed in its tracks. Here is some practical advice on handling the "middles":

- Identify the informal leaders within middle management and where their executive support resides and determine their real span of influence
- Get to know them by listening and figuring out what makes them tick (and what's making them ticked)
- Up front you need a vocal minority that accepts the change; continue to communicate openly; work at bringing more middle managers into the fold
- Don't get too stressed out by the stragglers because as momentum for integration builds, and they continue to object, their single mindedness will lead to their own demise (a wonderful example of a self-fulfilling prophecy)

Keeping organizational politics in the back of our minds, we need to go deeper and describe a number of critical performance indicators we use to align sales and service to get and keep the *right* customers.

CHAPTER 6—WANTING THE SAME THINGS II

Nothing so needs reforming as other people's habits.

Mark Twain (***Pudd'nhead Wilson, 1894***)

C ustomers are a capital investment, so it's critical for every company to determine whether they can expect to receive a reasonable return on their sales and service investments before they commit to a customer. It's equally important for a business to know whether they are garnering that ROI with its current customer base.

Remember,

> All customers are not created equal.

Evaluating a customer's economic worth is good business.

DETERMINING CUSTOMER VALUE AND PROFITABILITY

It starts with gathering and analyzing specific financial data about current customers. The ability to calculate customer worth immediately is dependent on the quality of financial and customer information. Experience suggests the available data will be wanting; however, we are confident most businesses can gather enough reliable information to do some basic customer analysis. Going forward, management can take some time to identify the additional data requirement to have more precise figures at its disposal.

There are several baseline customer measurements every organization should gather and track. Capturing customer retention figures is common; but many firms don't look beyond this rudimentary benchmark. Knowing that a customer defected is one thing, but there are other critical elements that go into understanding the true nature of the discarded relationship.

- How long was the customer relationship
- What was the customer's financial contribution to the business
- Why did the customer choose to leave

To calculate a customer duration number, the firm must compare the customer start (assuming it's captured) to end dates and capture the difference in time. Duration figures can be further honed by testing different time periods to determine whether it produces interesting defection trends. For example, what percentage of new customers (those acquired within the last year) defected? How does that number compare to customers that defected at three, five and ten years? That takes care of the duration question.

Next, generate a report that indicates departing customers' purchase history and extrapolate past buying behavior to estimate revenue loss. This measurement is a powerful tool because it puts a value face on the customer. It's one thing to review a report that says a customer left. It is eye-popping when a report indicates that customer generated Y in revenue during the previous twelve months and the lost revenue opportunities in the future.

Understanding why customers really leave is the final piece of the puzzle. An arms length exit survey doesn't cut it. We have urged executives to personally call <u>former</u> customers who once did significant business with the company. Despite the perceived embarrassment and the uncomfortable nature of the conversation, it is imperative that executives hear customer feedback directly. In most cases, no one ever bothered to ask customers why they left, that must be the first objective of the conversation. The second objective (which was contingent upon whether the problem was fixable) was to see if there was some way to mend the broken relationship. In addition to getting an unfiltered read on various customer issues, in thirty (30%) percent of the cases the executives were able to reestablish the relationship and bring the customer back into the fold. Once the firms start to recognize the importance of measuring customer value, the next step is to segment customers by profitability.

SEGMENTING CUSTOMERS BY PROFITABILITY

The task at hand is to categorize existing customers into three categories. Using the airline industry's example of first-class, coach and economy, we can clearly identify a customer's value to the organization and determine how each customer segment must be treated. Perhaps the simplest label, however, is to identify customers as "A," "B" and "C."

The facts we are about to share with you are disturbing. [If a Valium™ [15] or other nerve pill is handy, take it before continuing. Otherwise remain seated and suspend your disbelief]. When we cited Pareto's Rule earlier to describe customer profits, we didn't present the whole story:

- **"A"** customers are the most profitable, encompassing those that fall in the top twenty (20%) percent (or less) of your existing customer base. This group typically produces eighty (80%) percent of total profits.
- **"B"** customers are those marginally profitable customers that represent approximately twenty (20%) percent to forty (40%) percent of your client base. They produce around fifteen (15%) percent of profit.
- **"C"** customers are the leftovers. Representing forty (40%) percent to sixty (60%) percent, "Cs" produce about five (5%) percent of the company's profit. [16]

As further validation, we have confirmed these percentages ± 5% percent with every one of our clients wherever we have conducted this analysis. Even our own client profit matrix looked like this at one time. Now, pay particular attention to the relationship between the size of each customer class and the group's combined profit output. While the 80/20 figure for "A" customer is problematic, the

---

[15] Valium is a Hoffman-LaRoche, Inc. trademark for the tranquilizer drug diazepam.

[16] Ness, Joseph A., Schroeck, Michael J., Letendre, Rick A., Douglas, Willmar J. *"The Role of ABM (Activities Based Management) in Measuring Customer Value."* <u>Strategic Finance Magazine</u>. March, 2001.

facts surrounding "C" customers are downright scary. How can a customer segment represent such a large percentage of the firm's base and have such little impact on profit? Consider these additional facts regarding the profit contribution of customers:

- "A" customers, on average, receive only twenty (20%) percent to thirty (30%) percent of a company's attention as reflected by time, effort and resources
- When "A" customers are lost, they tend to be replaced with "C" customers because these are the easiest to acquire
- Losing an "A" customer has five to ten times the impact on profitability as losing a "C" customer
- "A" customers are the primary source of today's profits and, if retained, they are the main source of future business growth

These trends arise because companies attempt to treat all customers equally. Corporations waste so much time and money reacting to all customers' wants/needs and pursuing any new business that few resources are available to meet the needs of those customers who generate the greatest value to the business. Once equipped with this newfound knowledge, a firm can take decisive actions to reverse these circumstances.

DOWNSIZE YOUR CUSTOMERS

This is not a misprint. When two people embark on a relationship, both parties have high hopes that they will gain some value from the union. Under normal circumstances, if one party does not benefit from the relationship, he or she will move on in search of greener pastures. This tends not to be the case with "C" customers: both parties hang on to these relationships even though there is no inherent value to either party.

A number of our early clients decided to give "C" customers to new and green sales people. The thought was if such people could reestablish the relationship and service the customer, additional sales opportunities would result. The only thing this decision accomplished was to quickly turn a promising salesperson into a disillusioned one. Constant rejection takes a toll: less than three (3%) percent of these "leads" ever turn into an acceptable new sale. The moral of this story is that too much time has gone by — the original sale is a distant memory. Here are our suggestions for "moving on" with your "C" customers:

STEP 1. *Do your homework.* Make decisions based on your current business model. If the business was built on low cost, high volume transactions, don't use customer downsizing as an excuse to reinvent the company's credo (unless there's an acceptable market-based reason for doing so.)

STEP 2. *Double-check the customer segmentation data.* Then, conduct a detailed analysis of the "C" customer data that goes beyond the raw numbers. B-to-B companies must look at "C" customers who are associated with "A" or "B" customers — divisions of parent companies, owners of multiple business entities, referral customers, etc. Retail businesses should identify "household" relationships — individuals holding the same demographics details (mailing address, telephone number, etc.) Both illustrations attempt to minimize potentially embarrassing situations with good customers whom you want to keep. [If this data on customer interrelationships is not collected currently, do some data sorting for obvious correlations. Then make sure IT alters/adds fields to the appropriate database so the information can be gathered going forward].

STEP 3. *Do some internal public relations.* With the customer data in hand, you need to do a bit of PR work with sales. They will absolutely, positively hate the idea of downsizing any customer. They've been brainwashed throughout human history with a myth handed down from generation to generation that says, "There's no such thing as a bad sale." Give sales the data (and the assumptions used to generate the numbers.) Have sales review the "C" customers too. Inevitably, they will identify additional customer relationships that should not be disturbed and give legitimate reasons for maintaining others. Repeat the same process with those on the service side who have direct customer interactions. Not only will these actions refine the list of targeted "C" customers, but also involving sales and service in the process, it will promote acceptance of the plan. [Remember, they're the people who will field the questions from these customers].

STEP 4. *Don't go crazy.* Hone in on the "no-brainers" on the first purge. We have found that a company can eliminate ten (10%) percent to fifteen (15%) percent of its customer base quickly, with very little pain, fanfare or risk to either the company or the customer. There will be borderline "C" customers: those who are nominally unprofitable or at a breakeven point. You may decide not to terminate relationships unilaterally, but give these customers a choice to remain in the fold. The easiest way is to give customers an option by establishing a service charge when they fail to meet the minimum standards.

STEP 5. *Develop clear policy guidelines.* This policy must focus on two things: communicating the financial rationale for the downsizing and establishing financial standards going forward so history doesn't repeat itself. For example, devising minimum sales amounts and minimum standards for transaction activity or account/purchase order size will add real meat to the guidelines.

STEP 6. *Determine how customers will be notified and draft the language.* Be honest, clear and concise. For instance, when writing to a business client, lay out the business rationale: "...We are taking this action to allocate our resources in a more cost effective manner." [Interestingly, a few clients have used this opportunity to blame themselves; essentially saying it was the company's fault this happened because they disregarded the customer in the past. Some even pledged improved customer support to those customers not affected by the downsizing]. Remember to provide adequate notice when necessary and make sure you include a telephone number for any questions or feedback.

STEP 7. *Determine how the company will handle customer comments or complaints.* Before any customer notification goes out, decide (with input from sales and customer service) how to handle any questions, complaints, etc. For example, when should exceptions be made?

STEP 8. *Send out the notifications and repeat this effort semi-annually or annually.* Trust us. This is a liberating experience. Assuming the company is taking care of business, this "C" problem will get smaller and smaller.

Once the customer downsizing project is finished, it's time to turn your attention to implement actions that will ensure the business never finds itself in the same predicament. It begins and ends by changing selling habits.

PROFITABLE PROSPECTING

In 1996, Alan Greenspan invented the phrase, "irrational exuberance"[17] to describe the frenetic growth of the stock market in the mid '90s. His comments carried such weight that the stock market's unbridled, bullish optimism was shaken and a brief, volatile sell-off reverberated through Wall Street. From time to time Greenspan would invoke his axiom and each time his remarks had the same effect on the markets. The Federal Reserve Chairman—as CEO of the U.S. economy—was essentially saying to investors, "Stop!" the illogical, speculative behavior.

Sales people suffer from a similar "irrational exuberance" in their interactions with prospects. Even top producers don't hit a home run with every sales pitch; sometimes they have trouble reaching first base. Still, sales people are a persistent bunch so they'll do everything in their power to stay in the game. Often they justify the time and expense of the extended courtship of a budding prospect by using the "potential" defense. It goes something like this, "I know it's not a great sale, but this customer has a huge upside. Let me knock down the price, get them aboard and I'll work the account to generate the numbers we want." Another angle could read: "I know this deal's not our core business, but look at the size of the account. All we need is to make a couple exceptions to make this deal work." Now it's time for a little introspection:

---

[17] Federal Reserve Chairman Alan Greenspan coined the term "irrational exuberance" during a speech on December 5, 1996 at the annual dinner and Francis Boyer Lecture of The American Enterprise Institute for Public Policy Research, Washington, D.C.

- How often does the company make a commitment to a customer based on a salesperson's claim of revenue potential
- Does the firm subscribe to the view that a few little tweaks will lead to a profitable relationship
- How many times do the "exuberances" proclaimed about these customers pan out into "A" relationships

Plain and simple, these are instances of pure selling lust.

"A salesman...he's a man way out there in the blue, riding on a smile and a shoeshine...A salesman is got to dream, boy. It comes with the territory."[18]

Businesses get themselves in this situation, because they enable their sales people too much. It's time to be more selective, more discerning about future partners, where we yearn for a long-term relationship, full of loyalty (and profits!) Look beyond the initial sale and examine a customer's future potential value.

The goal of profitable prospecting is to identify the right customers from the start (and take some calculated risks on bona fide potential), thereby avoiding the heartache of committing to an unwarranted, unprofitable relationship. By analyzing prospects based on the bottom line as op-

---

[18] From Arthur Miller's play <u>Death of a Salesman</u>. (1949).

posed to top line potential, being conscious of early warning signs, and learning to say "No" in certain circumstances, an organization can avoid accumulating more "C" customers. The best way to provide the necessary objectivity is through customer acquisition cost analysis.

Let's start with a few basic ways to calculate acquisition costs across customers. While the following methods are not hard and fast, we do have a piece of advice: don't get so caught up in the details that you try to figure out costs to the penny. Tracking and allocating expenses could take on a life of its own—and pretty soon you find yourself with a cadre of accountants that cost the firm as much as several unprofitable customers. Opt instead for one of these less cumbersome methods:

- If the business sells its products or services directly to a large number of customers and/or individual new customers who cannot easily be identified, acquisition costs should be performed on an average cost basis. Take total selling and administrative expenses and divide the result into total number of customers.

- If the company sells its products or services indirectly through a sales force or other middleman and individual customers can be easily identified (and the numbers are not overwhelming), consider allocating costs to individual customers or using a combination of individual and average cost methods.[19]

---

[19] It's not uncommon to use a "hybrid" cost allocation system—distributing some costs individually while allocating other expense types on an average costs basis.

- Firms that sell high ticket and/or complex products or services—such as space rockets or high priced software—should always calculate acquisition costs per customer. Since these types of corporations incur acquisition costs whether or not a prospect turns into a paying customer and expenses vary prospect-by-prospect, there is more value separating acquisition numbers and not lumping all prospects into the same bucket.

Utilizing financial yardsticks such as a minimum sale standard, estimating revenue combined with the customer acquisition costs, provides management with the objectivity to dispassionately evaluate a prospective customer's relative worth using a rudimentary breakeven point and a long-term value calculation.

Use these numbers as guidelines—make people accountable to these factors, but don't become so married to them that it puts the sales force into such a tight box that they no longer take rational chances. Now that we have planned for the future relationship with our customers the organization must address its past sins.

STOP ENABLING LOSS LEADERS

Prospecting for profits goes beyond just the dollars and cents; it calls for sense—common sense. A loss leader sales strategy is touted as a means to introduce customers to your business via a bargain. For new businesses or new product categories, this can be an effective tactic. The loss leaders we run into are situations where the product/service was offered to a customer for a valid business reason; however, things are way beyond the "introduction" stage. Years have passed; all the time, money and resources that went into creating that product or service have little (if any) chance of providing profit to the organization. In other words, we're talking about "forgotten" lost leaders: think of them as nothing more than "C" customers magnified. They are "C" lines of business, special services, or exception processing. There are very easy explanations why these loss leaders came to be. Someone either:

- Didn't say "No" to a prospect
- Couldn't say "No" to an existing customer
- Should've said "No" or "Stop" to a senior executive

It's the same story, different characters. For sales, getting a prospect to say "Yes" means that they don't say "No." Some will go so far to say that "No" is not part of the sales vocabulary. The excuse for the service side is a bit more complicated. When they don't say "No" it's because they either didn't have the power or weren't given the opportunity to do so. If they did say "No" their input was likely discounted. Regardless, the service side usually gets stuck supporting the "loss leader" relationship.

To make matters worse, the senior team often acts as a true enabler by proudly maintaining the need for such relationships. For whatever reason, they allow the loss leader relationship to begin and they see untold value in its continuity. So (in many cases) millions of dollars, hundreds of people, and years of work, are used to support an unprofitable service, line of business or process. What can be done about this now, and how do we stop it from happening in the future?

Dealing with a loss leader "after the fact" is a tricky situation, because these products and services tend to be offered to the very customers we want to retain: "A" and "B" customers. We don't want to take any actions that will disenfranchise valued customers, so there are a number of variables to carefully evaluate:

- How did the loss leader emerge?
- What's the history?
- Who are (were) the key decision makers? Who are the customers and how are they impacted if the loss leader is eliminated?
- Where does the loss leader fit into the company's overall business scheme?
- Are there alternative products/services available to the affected customers?

We have successfully employed several different tactics to improve loss leader predicaments based on the answers to these questions. Here is a brief summary of each course of action:

Sell it. Generally this is where a "diversification" strategy has gone badly. If the customers and the product/service have no relationship or "synergies" to the company's primary business, selling the unit is the best (and luckiest) course of action. The sell decision is relatively easy. Finding a potential buyer, however, requires work. Even if the unit is not "investment banker material," there are plenty of reputable business brokers around who can nevertheless assist with the valuations and finding potential suitors.

Just stop doing it. It's common to find a company, particularly smaller businesses, that offered a product or service for a "potential" big core business customer. Time passed, the potential never materialized and the company is stuck with the daily drudgery of maintaining this service or product at a loss. Assuming it remains highly unlikely that this fringe client can be converted into a core customer, it's time to call it quits. Get familiar with any contractual arrangements, research possible alternatives (no bridge burning!) and contact the customer. Be completely honest — explain the rationale and the economics. The customer won't like what they hear, but our experience has been that, by speaking businessperson to businessperson, they come to begrudgingly respect the decision. Discuss options, negotiate sufficient notice and plan for the transition.

Leverage it. Outsource it. Or, **cost effect it.** These options are for those businesses that have no choice but to maintain the loss leader. The company has no choice because:

- The customers are important to the core business
- The customers expect the product/service to be offered
- The product or service rounds out your business line

Begin by researching whether the product/service can be leveraged beyond the narrow confines of today. Is there a viable market for this product/service? If so, determine what it would take in dollars and in resources to make it a winner. Obviously, the firm won't want to throw good money after bad; however, if the numbers are not prohibitive, go for it.

When trying to turn things around is not the practical solution, the outsourcing option may be an appropriate course of action. Outsourcing is not for everyone, especially for firms that are...well, control freaks. Culturally, some believe that no one else can do it better or with the same customer care. In this case, look to outsourcing businesses that allow the host company to maintain control over the customer relationship. Regardless, outsourcing is not to be taken lightly because the buck stops with your business. Do zealous due diligence, negotiate performance standards with "out" clauses and don't enter into a deal for more than one year. Be (keenly) aware of any adverse customer feedback and stay connected with the outsourcing partner.

The last resort is to make the loss leader more cost effective. Assemble a small project team with a mandate to get the loss leader to break even, or better yet, to make a small profit. Investing in a process reengineering effort or better technology integration can produce results that make the money losing unit more palatable.

The keys to prevent future loss leaders from springing up are straightforward. First, senior management and sales must know the limits of their organization's capacity to deliver. Since this information comes from the service side of the business, service is obligated to educate and to validate — and management is obligated to listen. If the reasons for offering a loss leader are compelling, try doing it on a pilot basis first. In the end, if the product or service has no value, someone must have the courage to say "No!"

Modifying old habits is never easy. Don't make the mistake of instituting all these great new practices and walking away happily assuming that because the emperor spoke, everything is fixed overnight. "So let it be written! So let it be done!" Only Yul Brynner can get away with a line like that. Therefore, you need to go to the next level in your quest for the perfect relationship. Senior management, the sales organization and the service organization need to communicate, to trust, to link and to coordinate — nurturing and supporting your customers.

CHAPTER 7—COMMUNICATING THROUGH TLC

The highest compact we can make with our fellow is—"Let there be truth between us two forevermore."

Ralph Waldo Emerson (The Conduct of Life, Behavior, 1870)

I t must be human nature that causes us to pour our hearts out to a best friend about the trials and tribulations we endure with our partner and yet never muster the nerve to tell that significant other the same thing face-to-face. There's a certain irony when the only courage we can marshal for communicating our true feelings lies behind the safety of a friend or a letter. We keep things hidden because we don't want the truth to hurt the feelings of a person we love. Sales and service keep secrets from each other, too; all be it, not because of love. Out of a need for power, for sheer sport, or laziness, sales and service don't communicate.

Hunkered down in their department fortresses, sales and service communication is at best barely perceptible or at worst clearly dysfunctional. As appalling as this sounds, we have come to understand that the lack of meaningful communication between sales and service is a learned behavior—handed down from executive to manager, from manager to employee. This vicious cycle not only damages customer relationships, it really hurts—business:

- Sales is uninformed about a big customer's potential departure
- Service says no to sales promises
- Service is caught unaware of a new product promotion
- Sales doesn't receive a hot lead
- Service is surprised by a changed delivery deadline

In case after case these everyday dealings are cloaked in secrecy and suspicion, with both sales and service using information as a power base; neither side sharing necessary information. Is it any wonder why sales and service have trouble communicating with customers?

THEY, THEM AND US

There is a foolproof way to discover whether your organization suffers from this malady. Walk around the office and listen closely to conversations. Take note of the types of pronouns used in these exchanges. How often do you hear the words "they," "them," or "us" as colleagues talk about rumors, specific incidents, other departments or business units or, for that matter, customers?

Employees do not use the terms "they," "them" and "us" with love and affection. Rather, they say these words with something more like animosity and malice. To illustrate, here are two sad, real world commentaries we've heard during client interviews:

- A service person stated with conviction, "My job is to save customers from them [sales people]!"
- A salesperson, speaking with a customer in our presence, "piled on" as the customer blamed and

denigrated the operational area for a problem. Not only did the salesperson openly agree with the customer, but added fuel to the fire by accusing "them [service area]" of a host of other transgressions.

Both sides are guilty of projecting negative attitudes toward each other and creating barriers to building meaningful internal relationships. Those attitudes also seep outside the organization's walls, preventing a company from building strong, lasting relationships with customers. Changing internal attitudes and assembling a healthy communication network is central to building trust and long-term relationships.

THE EFFECT ON "THEM"

Throughout the book we've used the phrase "sales promises" to symbolize the unwritten contract with customers. These promises are vital to long-term business success. They are a critical corporate responsibility—a true customer advocacy. Sales guarantees that the customer's needs, both routine and non-routine, will be met by the company's product or service. The customer ultimately makes his/her decision to buy (or not to buy) based on the trust they believe that these promises can be met. Whether we look at activities such as an institutional money manager's buy/sell decisions in the equity markets, or the purchasing behavior of a suburban soccer mom for a SUV, final judgments rest on the level of trust they have in the company's ability to meet their needs.

We believe that breakdowns in communication between sales and service cause the corporation to renege on its promises, which ultimately destroys customer trust. Many businesses live insecurely within a glass house built on perceived trustworthiness; soon to be pummeled by the stones of possible local outrage carried by mere word of mouth or a full-blown national scandal sensationalized by the media.

An investment management firm with which we are familiar, bearing an impressive track record that spans over two decades, ran into a word of mouth hurricane. It held a conservative, value-based philosophy; its stated investment objectives were to minimize risk and preserve capital. The sales force was in the difficult position of touting strategies not in vogue during the go-go nineties. We're all aware how the stock market acted in those halcyon days, recording double digit gains as it rode the technology bubble. The mania was particularly impressive over the second half of the 1990s. The more stock prices raged ahead, the louder the investment firm raised red flags — warning that stocks were over-valued and that a market correction was due. So to protect gains, our example firm moved more and more assets out of stocks and into cash. However, when the market didn't correct, those who sold the firm's services started at first whispering, then yelling that the firm had lost its edge; its investment philosophy no longer applied to the new economy. Even the firm's senior management began to question its investment approach. These opinions made it out to the investors and they began demanding that the company change and allow them to partake in the high returns everyone else was enjoying in the market. Yet, despite the continued gains, the firm held securely to what they knew was the correct strategy: preserve capital. As more and more people talked, more and more clients liquidated assets. By the time the bear market correction officially began in March 2000, the business had lost over seventy-five (75%) percent of its assets under management. In short, the company experienced the devastation caused by bad internal word of mouth.

Yet more recently we witnessed the national media obsession over the sudden decline and fall of Arthur Andersen. Some want us to believe that Andersen's ruination was caused by the actions of a few "rogue" partners when, in our opinion, we can trace the disaster back to a culture where sales considerations became more important than the firm's core business. Maintaining a transparent, arm's length relationship with a client no longer served as the litmus test that enabled the firm to independently audit clients' financial statements. Partners were more concerned with "keeping clients happy" by telling them what they wanted to hear, and not the truth. Not making waves during audits ensured that lucrative consulting assignments remained safe and secure.

In the first example, customer perceptions became the reality. The latter demonstrates how honest communication can be seen as some kind of impediment to progress and wealth. In either case the results were the same; customers broke faith with the companies and reacted decisively with their feet.

These examples are only extreme in that they represent a <u>swift</u> customer reaction. Usually when conflicting communication between sales and service break customer trust, corporations die a slow, painful death — one customer at a time. The long-term success of sales and service integration is predicated on bringing the program into the trenches and we begin this process by attending to the health of the company's internal communication system.

BREAKING DOWN BARRIERS WITH TLC

Our clients have achieved a healthy, integrated sales and service communication network with our three-pronged **TLC** method. Now don't fret...we certainly realize that sales and service types would not tolerate sitting around in small groups, getting in touch with their feelings and attempting to relate to one another as sensitive men and women! The letters in this case don't carry their traditional meaning. Our TLC stands for <u>Trust, Linkages</u> and <u>Cohesion</u>. We're not going to get overly touchy-feely. Our version of TLC offers genuine deliverables.

We start our campaign through communication and training that focuses on preparing the staff for change. The program we use for managing change is pretty standard fair so we're not going to spend time chronicling it. Yet, we have one word of caution to senior management: even when you dutifully schedule your employees to attend change readiness seminars, your obligation does not stop there. Real effective readiness training requires regular maintenance, because employees need constant reassurance about the future as the integration initiative unfolds.

For a variety of reasons, people fear the uncertainty associated with change; traditionally, change workshops only serve to heighten employees' suspicions. With their eyes and ears wide open, employees continually scan the landscape for any signs of negative events—real or imagined. Uncertainty is bad enough; surprises are devastating to an organization's psyche. Therefore, senior management must remain vigilant to ensure a bolt from the blue (whether real or not) does not derail the initiative. In short:

- Constantly communicate the business rationale for integration
- Continually reinforce the company's objectives for

the program
- Elaborate on the progress, affirm milestones small and large, and celebrate triumphs along the way

Use each opportunity to build trust. Be honest and straightforward in all your communication, don't evade peoples' questions, don't be afraid to say, "We don't know the answer, but we'll find out and get back to you soon." While employees won't always like everything said, they will come to respect the integrity of the messages.

COMMUNICATING TRUST

In order for our model to succeed, one item is critical above all others: an organization must hold trust in the highest esteem. As we've previously explained, trust must exist between the organization and its employees, between business units, and between the customer and the company. Our program shows that a meaningful trust environment begins with building mutual respect between sales and service; consequently, we have developed a workshop designed to adjust the misconceptions and the myths that sales and service hold about each other:

- The service organization believes that, "We do all the work." They believe sales folks hold stress-free jobs, earning big money entertaining prospects—playing a round of golf, having a few cocktails and a nice meal, and talking a little business in between.
- The sales organization states, "Without us, you wouldn't get a paycheck." They believe the service folks have the stress-free jobs; lounging around in meetings, fielding personal calls while occasionally moving some-

thing from the "in" bin to the "out" bin.

THE WORKSHOP EXPERIENCE. The training process begins with an appreciation of the expertise and "sameness" between sales and service by "walking a mile in each other's shoes." Both sides come to realize that the other has its share of job woes. The service world recognizes that business travel is not chic, but filled with the frustrations of long lines, cold calls, flight delays, cancelled appointments, missed family activities, countless presentations, writing proposals, "in your face" rejections and reams of mind-numbing paperwork. Sales becomes familiar with actual work volumes, customer complaints, computer crashes, tight deadlines, missed family activities, the get-nothing-done meetings, office politics, internal bureaucracies, and reams of mind-numbing paperwork.

The class then examines what it takes to be successful in either discipline. Coming in, most service people perceive themselves as not having the skills or personality to sell and sales people feel they don't have the temperament or inclination to dig into the details. By steering discussions around what it's really like to identify prospective customers, make initial sales calls and negotiate contract terms as well as working within high volume bureaucracies, defusing irate customers, and navigating office politics, the participants start to see each other's work through one lens.

As we establish some common ground, we then explore real life situations that illustrate the ways sales and service may impede each other's work. For example, inevitably the sales people want to discuss why the service organization always appears to say "No" whenever sales puts a special request on the table. There is a noticeable tone of frustration in the sales folks' voices as they give details of lost sales because service invoked a particular rule or hid behind a system constraint to nix the deal. Middle managers from both sides quickly put forward the corporate line. Service types rationalize, interject and defend their position by forecasting the apocalyptic consequences of accepting the exception. After much finger pointing and soul searching, someone in the audience offers a solution to the quagmire. The motion is debated—sometimes heatedly—but on the whole it's a healthy dialogue. This often represents the first time these groups have communicated in an adult manner. As tempers ebb, other thoughts are proposed: technology issues, delivery timeframes, the necessity for certain paperwork, and even how each group interprets terminology differently. Slowly the momentum shifts, there's less defensiveness and the two sides actually begin operating in solution mode.

COMMUNICATING "LINKAGES"

Once a real dialogue begins and the self-awareness is established, the next phase of building trust occurs. As with any intimate relationship, bonding is a powerful means of communication in its own right. We make this important connection by bringing a small number of sales and service folks together on a team. This project team has one goal: construct a "seamless" customer handoff from sales to the rest of the organization—without a glitch and in a way that is invisible to the customer. In other words, the customer falls in love, goes to bed and wakes up in the morning feeling as if they're still with the same person. In addition to these marching orders, we indoctrinate the team using selected topics on basic process redesign and team building to give the group the necessary skills to accomplish their mission.

THE PROJECT TEAM EXPERIENCE. Every business maintains a series of mechanisms to move the customer through the organization. This infrastructure is part of service's domain. There are plenty of architects of the service "box," a device designed to accommodate customer needs as service sees them. This container is filled with all kinds of paraphernalia: forms, computer systems, manual processes, practices and policies. In addition to the tangible network, there's also the matter of how the responsibility for the customer relationship is transitioned from one side of the business to the other. The project team embarks on its odyssey by examining whether the service box is actually designed to work effectively with sales and the customer.

How often does the customer's business reach the service organization correct and ready for processing? From experience, that percentage is always underestimated. Here's a case in point. While conducting an assessment for a client, we recognized that there was a customer handoff problem. It wasn't hard to discern because things were bad enough for management to institute a "bounce back" procedure. In other words, when a service person received a contract from sales that was not ready for processing, they gave it to their manager, who in turn, gave it to the sales manager. The bounce back report indicated that fifteen (15%) percent of all contracts were returned in this manner. During interviews with some service people, they informed us that the actual contract rejection number was more like thirty (30%) percent to forty (40%) percent. They underreported the instances because if they followed the written bounce back procedure, the customer order would be delayed by some two weeks as the contract bounced back and forth between peoples' desks. As it turned out, the service folks either fixed the problem themselves or dealt with the salesperson directly to get what they needed to fulfill the customer request.

In another example, we had a client who could not account for bad customer paperwork. Through observation we identified an underlying cause: the front-line folks said that fifty (50%) percent to sixty (60%) percent of the customer orders they received were incomplete. Senior management, in their infinite wisdom, felt the issue was minor; five (5%) percent to maybe ten (10%) percent of new business was incomplete. Not to be outdone, middle management cited a figure of around twenty (20%) percent. We had the staff track all new business for two weeks to get a better sense of things. It turned out that just over fifty (50%) percent of the paperwork was incomplete. As if this wasn't bad enough, seventy (70%) percent of the rejected orders required the salesperson to contact the customer to fix the mistake! Realize that in both illustrations, these paperwork troubles were not customer exceptions but a part of normal, routine purchases.

Once the group understands both the primary reasons and the extent for the process missteps, they are set to make things right. Many of the solutions are easy to identify and fix: less and clearer paperwork, easier to understand computer screens, more agile manual processes and smarter policies. After the group tackles the routine issues, they must deal with exceptions. Those instances where the service box alone cannot solve the problem.

What role do "exceptions" play in the process? What is the effect of exceptions on the infrastructure? This question must be investigated thoroughly. Small and mid-sized businesses as well as companies in niche markets need to be particularly diligent in evaluating exceptions. Not only is it likely that these businesses see more instances for special handling, it may be to the point where exception processing is more the rule, than the exception.

Firms in this situation face a serious predicament—their infrastructure is overly complex. The box makers, in an attempt to devise a well-oiled machine, built standard procedures filled with unyielding, multi-part decision rules to accommodate every situation. The mistakes and delivery delays that result become broken sales promises. Part and parcel to the handoff, the group must also tackle the vexing issue of maintaining customer accountability through the transition.

Who should be responsible for the customer relationship transition from sales to service? Before a sale is closed, everyone knows with certainty that sales is responsible for the customer relationship. Once the deal is done, however, a state of ambiguity prevails. Sales only knows that they are no longer responsible for the customer. The customer is unaware of any transition—not because the customer doesn't know that they've been transitioned—innately they do. They just don't know to whom. Sadly, this is usually true of the service organization as well. Naturally, the service organization <u>knows</u> it is responsible for solving customer problems, filling orders, and answering questions. Yet they don't believe that they have true control over the one-on-one customer relationship. When everyone is responsible, no one is accountable; therefore assigning accountability for the customer relationship becomes an impossible task. We've employed the following solutions to transfer accountability to the service organization. The key factors the team must consider include:

- The size, variability and complexity of the sale
- The service infrastructure currently in place to respond to the above elements
- Transaction volume

- Resource alignment and the structure of sales and service units

In business situations where there is less intricacy, we have utilized a simple customer "contact" system. There is nothing more powerful than making the transition a personal, face-to-face experience. For example, when the sale is conducted at the company's office, we recommend that sales people actually introduce the customer to the key service contacts. It can be accomplished with a tour of the facility that includes personal introductions.

In other circumstances, we require an individual from the service side to contact the customer personally. The staff person introduces him or herself and informs the customer that they have received their order and they are the person responsible for ensuring its completion. Then they verify the specifics of the transaction and validate when it will be delivered. They close the call by providing a direct means for the customer to reach them if they have questions or concerns.

For firms that have advanced workflow technology in place, designing a customer contact module makes the most sense. Some e-businesses effectively use a series of e-mails to alert the customer of the order's progress as it moves through to fulfillment. Brick and mortar companies can employ the same idea with a telephone call, fax or e-mail.

A word of caution is needed here. Don't fall into the automation trap — washing one's hands of the customer — and assume the "system" will take care of everything. When things run smoothly, a preset system is fine, but should a snag occur, all an automated message (or the absence of one) does is encourage the customer to make a call to the customer service unit. Beat the customer to the punch! Have a real person contact them to explain the difficulty, offer alternative solutions and reach a consensus for moving forward. A swift response that mitigates a potential problem is a sure way to turn a bad situation into a loyalty-building event.

Finally, for companies with more involved transactions and a more sophisticated product/service delivery structure, such as: technology deployment, professional services, service bureaus, or acquisitions (i.e. sales situations where a customer's existing business is acquired), we have had tremendous success deploying "C.A.T.s" — also known as customer acquisition teams.

THE C.A.T. EXPERIENCE. Like the customer contact systems, the primary purpose of the C.A.T. team is to transition accountability for the customer from sales to service. Its secondary aim is to assist sales to close deals. As a consequence, service must learn the specific needs of a new customer in order to prepare the service infrastructure to "execute and deliver" on the terms of the sale.

Whether the C.A.T. team is installed as a permanent entity, a sub-group of a department or an ad hoc unit is contingent on the scope and frequency of new customer acquisitions. Regardless of the structural approach, it's critical that the C.A.T. team be fully integrated with the mainstream service organization. We strongly recommend that the team be staffed with multi-disciplinary talent. In addition to sales representation, the team needs the appropriate expertise from those units integral to carrying out product/service delivery. An even more important factor than the team's collective know-how is its psychological make up. It must be manned by "can do" problem solvers. Lastly, the team's reporting relationship must be high enough to guarantee that team decisions become reality.

Ideally the C.A.T. team (or a senior representative of the unit) is brought into the picture during the latter stages of the sales process. Initially, the unit will provide general and detailed educational sales support—addressing a prospective customer's specific questions and concerns relating to product/service delivery. On other occasions, they act as problem solvers, working through alternatives and solutions to meet a prospective customer's particular needs (read exceptions.)

Once the deal is closed, the C.A.T. group goes into overdrive. They meet directly with the new customer to understand first hand the business needs. From there, the group moves onto implementation matters, solving problems and performing the work necessary to bring the customer "on board" and integrating them into the mainstream service organization. We have also observed that as C.A.T. teams become more experienced, they "franchise" transition tactics by creating detailed work processes, checklists, system interfaces, reports and other tools.

By way of illustration, for a service bureau client we formed multiple C.A.T. teams that were small, sub-groups of the regional units responsible for supporting customer transactions. In this variation, the C.A.T. staff was the customer's initial service contact that worked with the customer to transition their business into the larger department. With a technology client we opted for permanent C.A.T. people that completed the initial installation and customer training, then facilitated help desk support and other post implementation services on behalf of the customer. Regardless of approach, the service contact provided the company with the first tangible mechanism to perpetuate the customer relationship beyond the initial sale.

COMMUNICATING "COHESION"

Once we have initiated a company wide dialogue that lays the foundation for trust and we have established the initial linkages to get sales and service to work together, we need to focus on efforts that build lasting integration. The goal is to have the service organization act as sales people and sales people to act like service providers. By supplying sales people and front-line service people with the skill sets to put our integration principles into action, we create cohesiveness among the employees who work directly on the customer front-lines.

THE FRONT-LINE EXPERIENCE. Sales and service staff attend the sessions together. Another feature of this training is its unconventional design. The program is developed to intentionally utilize class "experts." By using certain training participants as the experts, it reduces resistance to the workshops and ultimately to the initiative as a whole. Lastly, these are hands-on, skills based sessions tailored to address the kinds of customer interactions the participants face daily.

We address the shared skills used by both disciplines. For example, both sales and service people use many of the same communication tools such as empathy, paraphrasing and summarizing. We do this intentionally to show that there is less of a professional "divide" as some may presume. Next, we address key topics to strengthen the skills of one group or the other. For example, we compare the difficulties of service listening techniques on the telephone to the advantages of sales listening in face-to-face situations. Service people are required to listen more closely because they do not have the advantage of observing a customer's non-verbal communications in determining a customer's real intent. We transfer these active listening skills to sales people; with improved listening, sales folks ask probing, customer-centric questions to understand the real needs of customers.

On the other side, we train the service organization to recognize and act on sales opportunities. This is not a small task because service types typically shy away from any selling situation. We get them comfortable with some of the basics first: gathering and pre-qualifying leads and actively soliciting referrals. In later sessions and as they build confidence, we introduce various selling concepts, ultimately working up to when and how to propose a new product/service and closing a sale with an existing customer.

Conversely, sales begins to realize that selling "service" is a powerful way to build confidence with prospective customers. Since customers (as well as prospects) look at the total experience and expect a business to live up to its promises, sales must incorporate the company's value-added benefits in their sales presentations. These value-added services are those elements of the company's infrastructure that sales can brag about to customers.

In this chapter we concentrated on the initial steps to coordinate sales and service activities that bring the customer into the organization seamlessly. Now we will examine those activities that build loyalty and retain customers over the long-term.

CHAPTER 8—WORKING AT IT

Perfection of means and confusion of goals seem — in my opinion — to characterize our age.

Albert Einstein (Out of My Later Years, 1950)

No relationship grows by maintaining the status quo. We have high expectations for ourselves and the people in our lives. We're always searching, always reaching, always moving forward. We want every time to feel like the first time. Business relationships are no different. We can take nothing for granted. We must work hard. Be creative. Innovate. Experiment. Create opportunities and fulfill our customers' every expectation and then some.

This chapter outlines the purposeful actions that build loyalty by reinforcing the customer's original purchase decision so he or she will not only want to do business, but do more business with your firm. Success breeds success.

CREATE CUSTOMER LOGIC

Organizations attempt to create logical systems and processes. Corporate designers translate this logic as serving internal goals in the most efficient, cost effective means possible. It's a natural reaction for employees (the designers) to create processes and systems that make things easier for them to perform tasks. The case of a former client stands as a good example for work practices that serve internal needs to the detriment of customers:

This firm is a financial institution that decided to do some cross-selling with its best small business customers. It sent out a terrific "...because you're a great customer you have been pre-approved" letter for a business loan. This letter motivated lots of customers to call for more information; however, very few loans were closed. Why? When customers learned what was involved with the "pre-approval process," they just said no thanks. As it turns out, the bank required the customer to submit all kinds information, that, for the most part the bank already had on file. The bank's "excuse" was that the customer data was not readily available. It resided in another department and, since a different business unit was handling the loan product, they had to collect it again for themselves!

In a customer-centric world, we turn things upside down. Systems and processes must be designed to:

Make it easier for customers to do business.

Identifying opportunities towards which to apply this credo is not complicated:

Minimize Paperwork. A guaranteed quick win in forming a customer-focused process is minimizing the paperwork (or computer interaction) a customer must execute. Paperwork is universally hated. Forms multiply like rabbits, computer screens proliferate like gremlins, and far too much of the information collected is superfluous. Whenever/wherever communication breaks down, the makeshift solution of choice is to craft a new form or paint another screen. Don't think the solution is to simply reduce the number of forms by cramming the same fields into a different format with smaller fonts and near microscopic space for which to fill in information. Such forms are especially annoying—particularly if the customer is over forty and visually challenged. Instead, critically examine whether the company in fact needs all the information it collects, eliminate requests for duplicate data, cut "for internal use only" boxes, and force the lawyers to be clear and concise. [Remind them that "hereby" and "aforementioned" are not real words]! Also be sure to provide customers with clear instructions or on-line help screens. An easy way to test the usability of your forms is to have a brand new employee complete the material. If they can't do it right, chances are neither can your customers. When all else fails, consolidate (i.e. make multi-use forms) and pre-fill those fields requiring standard information.

Streamline processes and operating procedures that directly impact customers. When customers must navigate through a process, ask two fundamental questions:

1) What is a customer required to do to get things acccomplished?
2) Why is the customer required to do it?

Assessing the impact a process or system has on a customer is not always evident. Sometimes you need to dig a bit. If error or quality reports on processes are available, they are a good starting point to determine if or where customer pitfalls exist. In particular, pay attention to "bounce backs"; those places in the process where work is rejected by one group and sent back somewhere (it need not be to the customer) for correction. These types of process problems—the cases that delay customer delivery—provide the perfect segue to discuss the next issue.

Reduce customer cycle times. This is the time it takes for the organization to get the product/service into the customer's hand. Whether or not you promise a specific delivery date, time (especially in these wired, information-rich days) is a tremendous premium for customers. They want their stuff delivered now, if not sooner. Minimizing the time it takes to accomplish tasks that have a direct bearing on customer deliverables is a sure-fire way to keep them coming back for more.

To reduce customer cycle times, we recommend a global approach. Scan the entire process. Understand the objectives for each stage as well as the controls, interconnections and handoffs as the process moves from person to person/department to department. Then conduct a detailed evaluation of every component by observing the people who do the work. Ask many "Why?" questions, and pay particular attention to the places in the organization/process where there are high levels of specialization. Evaluate whether technology interfaces support or slow manual processes. Talk about the problems they encounter and be sure to discuss exceptions. Determine where and how the customer fits into the picture; what customer interaction takes place (telephone, written correspondence, etc.) If there is no customer interaction as a part of the process, should there be?

Now take out a clean piece of paper and:

- *Reduce the number of "touches."* Typically more time is wasted as the paper/widget moves from desk to desk.
- *Abolish or minimize specialization.* This is a powerful solution. It saves time. Employees become smarter whenever they learn/know the entire process, and

this simultaneously makes them accountable and empowered. Since there's no one else to point fingers at, they must take responsibility to get things right.

- *Eliminate excessive controls.* If there is more than one quality check (formal or informal) either the wrong people are doing the work, or a bad situation — some historical anomaly — transpired and extra controls were put in place years ago to make certain it never, ever, ever happened again.
- *Remove other work redundancies or unessential tasks*

Once the excesses are eliminated from the procedures and systems supporting the customer, the entire process must be tied together by addressing the following:

- *Add customer contact points.* Find places to update customers as to the status of their order. A quick call or two along the way builds confidence that your business is on top of things and gives customers the feeling that they are important.
- *Redesign technology applications, paperwork, etc. to support the new process.* Be sure the user is in control of these efforts. Even though the term "user-friendly" is bantered about, many Information Technology units are still under the misguided notion that users should get applications that IT thinks they need or want.
- *Test and refine the new processes.* Train a pilot team to test the new processes and systems. Not only will the pilot people work out any bugs, but they will also discover better ways to make things more customer-centric.
- *Document, train and implement.* This work is often

performed in a shoddy manner or neglected entirely. Don't make the same mistake. Otherwise, employees will take those new, customer-centric practices and change them back to the old ways of doing things.

Improve written customer communications. Customers are also affected by any written communication the company generates. Those who have dabbled with writing love letters know full well that the written word can frequently make or break a relationship. Reevaluating computer "output" customers receive is a prime target for improvement. Is the information clear? Concise? Intuitive? In other words, does the customer construe the same meaning from the material as the company intends?

Review account statements and invoices. Pay particular attention to these two items because internal needs tend to supersede customer needs. We have seen numerous examples where a client's invoices ranged from the simply careless, to the vague and/or intentionally misleading. This ambiguity can have a far-reaching negative impact on the business.

On the surface, one of our clients had a growing and successful business with great cash flow. The second week of every month, however, there was this unexplained spike in customer deflections. The problem was ultimately traced back to their customer billing practices. Customers were billed annually based on information gathered manually from the firm's strategic partners. The strategic partners had no vested interest in the validity of the data; mistakes and inconsistencies were commonplace, and the company accepted the data on blind faith. [The company also had no way to tell that the figures were bad]. The end result was invoices that were unclear and/or flat out wrong. Even in the best of circumstances, the customers did not have enough information on the statement to check the math. The invoices were mailed on the last business day of every month. Customers would review the statement, become confused, or more likely, get mad and call customer service. The service representatives tried to defuse the situation. Seventy (75%) percent of those who complained canceled the service. Another group of customers ignored dunning letters, withheld payment and quietly took their business elsewhere. The moral: make certain account and billing statements are clear, easy to read and always correct. Keeping customers is tough enough; self-inflicted transgressions are simply inexcusable.

Review other forms of written communications: letters, e-mails, marketing brochures. These materials can cause unintended consequences, too. Our favorite anecdote is the client who established an "advisory alert" process to provide its customers with "up to the moment" notification of its portfolio investment position. The firm used a "blast fax" (this was in the days before e-mail) to get the word out to customers. There was only one small problem. Someone had the "bright idea" of sending the transmission out using a red background with black text. This continued for three months before someone in the company realized that customers were receiving a black facsimile copy. To our knowledge, the company's customers never found out who was responsible for the black fax — it was a closely guarded corporate secret. Nonetheless, we have to admit that the manager responsible for this folly took the term "techno-neophyte" to a whole new level.

MOJO LOGIC

There's an aura that surrounds technology, a magic that has even entered into the realm of relationships. Just imagine how much more "free love" would have been consummated in the 1960s had computer dating services and Internet chat rooms existed as they do today. Business has realized countless efficiencies and productivity gains because of new technologies. With much of a company's internal systems in place, more and more customers are coming in direct contact with a company's computer systems, e-business applications and other thingamabobs. While we are strong advocates for new and better technology, it gets tricky when companies want to utilize it exclusively for customer interactions.

Our trepidation starts these self-proclaimed "user-friendly" folks. They talk a good game, but based on the multitude of self-described "friendly" software applications we've evaluated, we shudder just thinking about letting them loose on unsuspecting customers. We've seen too many technology initiatives that only serve to turn off prospects and push existing customers to competitors. As a result of these experiences, we developed 10 points to guide customer-focused technology:

- *Point 1. Technology is an enabler.* It is not a cure-all. It won't compensate for inefficient processes, or fix poor sales or service delivery, or camouflage staff incompetence.
- *Point 2. Watch out for the "Field of Dreams" syndrome.* If we build it they will come... There are far too many examples where companies invest in technology solutions that flat out fail. Don't assume you know what customers want.
- *Point 3. Do your homework.* Determine your primary

120

objectives and business requirements. Devise realistic budgets, payback forecasts and project plans through to implementation. Ask the right questions and check the numbers twice. We've seen more than our share of creative forecasting. [20]

- *Point 4. Know the computer literacy of projected customers.* It's a mixed bag: some customer segments are fully "wired," but there remains a large segment that doesn't (or won't) use computers and still others that have limited techno savvy.
- *Point 5. Solicit customer feedback early and often.* Use this as an opportunity to ask customers to analyze and improve the application's design. Be discriminating. Beside great ideas and honest feedback, lookout for unrealistic requests or expectations.
- *Point 6. Keep customer computer interactions simple and "idiot proof."* The greater the system's complexity, the more likely customers will experience problems.
- *Point 7. Eliminate all instances of "internalese" and jargon from the system.* Some companies have a tendency to simply make or convert internal systems for customer use and assume they can use it.

---

[20] The Gardner Group, a technology consulting firm surveyed Fortune 500 CEOs regarding the effectiveness of technology in their organization. As reported in a 1998 Wall Street Journal article, the survey respondents indicated that over forty (40%) percent of the technology initiatives instituted in the last three years were not implemented. Another twenty-eight (28%) percent were scaled back due to cost and schedule overruns. The CEOs went on to say that even when technology systems were implemented, in most cases, seventy-three (73%) percent, the systems did not achieve the efficiencies and benefits originally promised.

- *Point 8. Test your site using the technology "interface" your customers use.* Many customers may not have T-1 lines or broadband access. Learn how most customers will view and experience the technology and test the applications using those parameters. If your application is too slow or graphically complex for customers, you'll know it and have time to fix it before you launch.

- *Point 9. Create integrated service delivery.* Don't repeat the "dot com" mistakes. You are looking for trouble if new technology processes (back-end) are different from your brick and mortar delivery systems.

- *Point 10. Incorporate a "human safety valve."* A good help function and tutorial are great starts, but make sure customers can get in touch with a real person to answer questions and handle problems.

In the end, good processes and systems deliver good sales and service, but they represent only half of the loyalty building equation. Coupled with a strong business infrastructure, sales and service must also produce an emotional connection with customers. Those feeling responses are the cement that keep customers coming back.

MAKE AN EMOTIONAL CUSTOMER CONNECTION

Every customer wants to feel that a company's products/services are beneficial and uniquely suited to meet their individual needs. Customers also want to feel that the organization focuses its attention on them constantly. These lofty expectations can be achieved without resorting to an all encompassing, costly, time-intensive business model.

SITTING BY THE PHONE

Most organizations approach service the way "renaissance" women of the 1960s approached dating. Imagine you meet the man of your dreams at the local dance and you give him your phone number. At the end of a wonderful evening, he promises to call and you go home in blissful anticipation of the next encounter. You can't wait until your dreamboat calls the next day. The next day comes and goes and lover boy hasn't called. So you sit by the phone and wait and wait and wait...

Businesses do the same thing. Sales brings in a new customer while the company spends wads of money to have people sit around by the telephone waiting for the phone to ring. When the telephone does ring, you react with the intent to keep your customer happy so they will come back for more. But what happens if the customer never calls?

We are not suggesting to board up service centers, it is necessary to "react" to customers. Making sure a customer's information requests are answered and their problems are solved is a basic customer expectation. What businesses must do is position those reactive services so they are delivered in an efficient and consistent fashion. This predictability leads customers to trust and depend on the organization. Here are several things the firm can do to encourage this confidence in customers:

Revisit Automated Attendant Usage. Businesses love the efficiency this service affords them. Organizations assume that the speed with which a call can be answered is an overriding need of all their customers. While customers need a quick response, they do not want to trade speed for the lack of human contact or an unproductive process. Customers hate inefficiency, especially impersonal inefficiency. The first step is to reassess whether use of the attendant fits with the image the company wants to present to its customers. For example, many boutique firms use customer intimacy as a selling point, so it is more appropriate to have a live person answer the telephone at all times. If you decide that an attendant is necessary to track and organize calls, be certain the message length and menu options are short and clear. Always have a "live person option" and we recommend stating that choice early in the message.

Create Meaningful Telephone Service Standards. These create the consistency and professionalism customers expect. Here's what to do:

- Start by getting front-line employees to greet callers in a consistent professional manner. Something like: "Good morning. Widgets R Us this is John Doe how may I help you?" Then develop scenarios covering how these employees should handle different call situations.
- Always answer the telephone within 3 rings, any longer and the customer starts to feel they are dealing with a company out of control (or worse — out of business.)
- Make it a practice for employees to pick up an unattended ringing phone.
- Always ask permission before placing a caller on hold. Tell them why and how long they will be on hold. If there's going to be further delay, get back on the phone and tell them.
- Never transfer a caller blindly. Make sure a person answers, and summarize the caller's issues before hanging up.

All of these situations are common telephone courtesies that are respectful of the caller's situation.

Voice Mail Standards. Voice mail is the next thing to tackle, because customers hate that, too. To mitigate customer resistance:

- Have *all* employees create a daily voice mail greeting. "Hi. You've reached John Doe's mailbox. Today is December 24th and I am in the office. Please leave your name, telephone number and a brief message and I will return your call shortly. If you need immediate assistance, please dial extension 555."
- Create a standard for returning voice messages. Never leave this standard up to employees since many tend to use voice mail to hide from customers.

Using Telephone Statistics. Larger organizations tend to manage customer calls through the use of statistical measurements.

- Track call types, monitor calls lost, hold times and call volume/by hour figures, and
- Throw out the rest of the reports

> Handling a customer's particular needs can't be neatly wrapped into a three-minute (on average) telephone call.

These suggestions are a crucial cost of doing business, but in the relative scheme of life, they have negligible long-term impact on the customer relationship. Customers have come to expect these types of reactive services. As a result, trying to build loyalty and cultivate the 3 Rs around reactive service is an exercise in futility and, unfortunately, these are the very services most companies rely on for just that purpose. They mistakenly think that providing great reactive service creates long-term loyalty! The firm must do more to influence customer feelings toward the organization. We refer to this customer outreach as "proactive" service.

PROACTIVE SERVICE

We have a question for all the women readers. [Guys...pay close attention]! So ladies, how do you feel when your special someone does something absolutely thoughtful, exceedingly wonderful without ever being asked? You feel treasured. You feel loved. You feel cherished. You feel respected, appreciated and valued. That's exactly what happens with proactive service—providing support and information without customers directly requesting it. The goal of proactive service is to turn things around and get customers to react to you. Proactive service is a tangible, persuasive and purposeful strategy.

First, anticipating is the foundation for proactive service. Customers say things to employees every day—things that can actually be seen—one just needs to learn where to look. It's a matter of "listening with your eyes." A customer calls to complain about a specific company practice. The telephone representative listens and effectively solves the problem. Call closed. This is a routine reactive situation. However, chances are others have the same complaint, but we never look at the practice beyond solving the particular situation unless it's catastrophic. Firms tend to leave well enough alone and not go looking for trouble. From our perspective this unwritten practice precipitates customer defections—in fact—ninety-six (96%) percent of customers who defect never call the company to complain.[21]

We recommend that firms should aggressively monitor and investigate complaints, specifically looking for trends. When you identify other customers with the same issue, fix the problem and then communicate the fix to the affected customers. Handling a situation before a customer realizes that there's an issue builds and maintains loyalty, because its shows accountability, responsiveness and—yes—caring.

Second, proactive service should add tangible value to the customer. Educate customers about current events that affect them: economic issues, industry topics, new products, etc. Notice we did not mention sales promotions in this sequence. Sending marketing material can be effective, but in the absence of other communications, it tends to get lost in the sea of snail mail or e-mail. Mixing in timely informational pieces, without an overt call to "buy me," becomes a service that broadens the customer relationship. Firms can also use proactive touches for other purposes.

Unpleasant public situations that surround your organization can create the real possibility that customers may jump ship, so communicate to retain. For example, when a company is in the center of a crisis, communicate early to calm and to reassure customers. Keep them informed through the process and remember to thank cus-

---

[21] The Technical Assistance Research Program. *"Customers Who Complain Are Really the Kind You Want."* The Record. January 13, 1999. TARP (Technical Assistance Research Programs), a U.S. group that focuses on complaining customers, found that only four (4%) percent of customers complain. Most go away angry and simply stop doing business with you.

tomers for their loyalty once things settle down. Day to day market conditions also afford the same opportunity. A case in point: firms in financial services have tremendous opportunities to be proactive. If, for example, the stock market (or a specific investment) is in the middle of a tumble, get a message out to customers like, "Stay disciplined, be patient... we're in this for the long-term..."

Third, proactive service can be used as a persuasive sales strategy. Information about future energy costs is a regular news staple. There may be a burst of press coverage over a change in crude oil production, perhaps the outgrowth of a recent OPEC meeting. With an impending price increase on the horizon, a heating oil business can send out a marketing piece offering the option to lock into a lower priced contract now before the price goes up. Maybe a supplier can send out a notice indicating that a product will be discontinued in thirty days. Proposing alternatives to the affected customers can immediately diffuse a situation that might otherwise encourage defection. When used regularly, not only do proactive services keep the company's name in front of customers, it is a tangible way to perpetuate the relationship—building loyalty and cultivating sales opportunities.

Fourth, proactive service is a purposeful strategy, particularly when it is targeted to meet the needs of specific customer segments, which leads us back to our A, B, and C customer classifications. Up to this point, we've described proactive service in general terms. The truth of the matter is that we are firm advocates of employing proactive services tactically by using different means and methods based on a customer's value to the organization. Let's circle back to the stock market illustration, this time using a tiered approach. During a market downturn, a stockbroker or financial advisor can communicate proactively by: calling "A" customers personally, having an assistant personally call "B" customers, and sending "C" customers a letter.

Even more important, a tiered proactive approach can also be applied strategically by tailoring the organization's resources and infrastructure. A company can decide that:

- "A" customers will receive more customized, personalized support
- "B" customers will be handled using turnkey and limited personal practices, and
- "C" customers will be educated on how to be more self-sufficient

Instituting a proactive scheme provides the company with an effective outlet to respond to any situation, which in turn offers true customer value.

"Working at it," demands that the organization come together to advance customer relationships — building loyalty to retain and resell. Changes to process, to technology and to sales and service delivery are necessary tactics; however, the implications of these changes must be considered. How should tasks be organized? How should resources be allocated? How can accountability be attained? In an integrated organization, these and other subjects, must be viewed in entirely new ways.

CHAPTER 9—TYING THE KNOT

Form and function are a unity... In order to enhance function, appropriate form must exist or be created.

Ida P. Rolf **(Rolfing: The Integration of Human Structures, 1977.)**

"S peak now or forever hold your peace." We have reached the stage of the process where decisions are to be made about jobs, reporting relationships, structure and power. "The family" is in uproar, unleashing a barrage of merciless comments on the prospects of a "wedding" between sales and service. Everyone has an opinion on the performance and effectiveness of the inner workings of the "other departments." Armchair critics within the company (you know who you are) sound off on the good, the bad, (and the ugly) aspects of the techniques, processes and methods relevant to the enmeshing of these business units in exactly the same manner as a "worried" bride "appraising" the character of her new mother-in-law.

While we understand that employees are reacting to the uncertainty caused by the impending nuptials, the company cannot become distracted by all the "emotional noise." It's time to tie the knot.

The decisions made will impact employees (and everybody knows it) and change the look of the company. Our approach to reshape jobs and structures is consistent from company to company, however, we must warn you there is no one-way to implement these strategies. Every company has its own quirks and idiosyncrasies that defy conventional definition, so the tactics for organizing and aligning people vary. The goal of this chapter is to help you navigate through the impact of integration on jobs, departmental functionality, and management structures by describing our methods and offering a series of "bottom-up" tactics we have used successfully to redesign jobs, reallocate resources and realign management.

JOB JUXTAPOSITION

Jobs must be reshaped and enriched. New roles are created and others eliminated. If there is one headline about integration and job formation, it's:

> Integration produces fewer workers who perform a broader range of tasks.

We begin by assessing the new, integrated processes, etc. and their relationship to current jobs—both roles with direct and indirect customer interaction. We have found that companies unconsciously look at these positions in an absolute manner—the activities and responsibilities are viewed in black and white. If the job does not require talking or writing to customers, it is labeled as an indirect position and any accountability to customers is erased. As a rule we look at the new integrated processes and determine where and how direct/indirect customer interactions should occur. Job responsibilities are shaped based on the logic of the system, not the conventional view of a particular job or functional department.

Jobs with direct customer contact are shaped to carry out both reactive and proactive service. Regardless of the type of customer interactions (i.e. face-to-face, voice or written), these positions are designed to maximize the customer's experience, creating a "personal feel" to the interactions. Let's look at three specific ideas:

For small and many mid-size businesses this can mean creating jobs responsible for sales and service related interactions. By making one job responsible for selling and servicing customers, there is a clear single point of contact, personalization and no relationship handoff. It's a powerful means to build customer loyalty and advance the 3 Rs.

Companies of any size can "personalize" the customer experience by incorporating simple (and easy) proactive customer interactions at various stages of the sales and service process. Inserting proactive touches into peoples' jobs is not hard — it just takes a bit of creativity. For example, a service unit can institute a practice where service representatives (not telemarketers) make follow-up calls to a certain number of customers to whom they spoke that day. In large call centers, give representatives the latitude to give out their direct extension to customers who inquired about difficult or complex issues. When a sales or service encounter necessitates that a form to be sent to the customer, the employee can call the customer a few days later to help the customer complete the paperwork.

Give authority to traditional "service roles" to have control over potential resale opportunities. During the course of a "service" call, the conversation turns into a sales opportunity. In most companies, the standard procedure is to have the service representative transfer the customer call to sales. In the thirty seconds it takes to transfer this call, the newly forged personal bond is broken and the sales opportunity lost. We are empowering employees to do things that move beyond the normal sales and service boundaries.

We further advance customer relationships by changing the orientation of jobs with indirect interactions. Regardless of the industry, market, or size, companies apply an assembly line mentality to jobs with indirect customer contact. Work activities are narrowly focused and exceedingly specialized. Employees that work in these highly concentrated roles only understand their little piece of the process. This is especially evident on the service side of the business where "efficiency" is the primary motivator in job (and process) design. In the name of productivity, managers force individuals to perform fragmented work. It's easier to direct, control and train employees who only do a little piece of a function. It creates a work world where jobs are "dummied-down" and, from our perspective, job specialization is a major contributor to the errors and delays customers encounter. To counter these issues, our redesign approach for indirect roles is to:

> Shape jobs with broader responsibilities and foster employee accountability by focusing on the *task inputs and outputs that affect customers.*

When work processes are redesigned and computer systems are refocused around the customer, job responsibilities change. A few years back we encountered a client where five specialists (housed in four different departments) handled a simple transaction. After a logical appraisal, we were able to collapse these five specialist jobs into two "generalists" and no one lost their job. Our preference is to have employees perform a process from beginning to end. By having "generalists" perform an entire procedure, employees get more meaningful, more purposeful work. [Often the job changes lead to higher pay, which can be afforded since there are fewer employees]. Management gets fewer, smarter, more productive employees who are genuinely accountable for their actions. Management gets the added bonus of greater resource flexibility.

Job specialization is actually more harmful than the "that's not my job" mentality. The trouble with job specialization is management's inability to move human resources where they are needed based on daily work volume. Routine events like "heavy mail day Mondays" or times when a business unit is short staffed because of a vacation, personal, or sick day, managers of a specialized workforce have little choice but to see critical work backlogged or left undone. If a department faces an extended absence, managers are forced to dole out overtime or requisition a temporary worker. With a unit of generalists performing the same functions from beginning to end, managers have the latitude to reallocate staff to cover an absence or to support a sudden explosion of work in another area. Shaping generalist roles for indirect service positions is an effective, powerful management tool.

Finally, there is the matter of integrating the professional and administrative staff. Information technology and accounts receivable are two such examples. It always astounds us when we encounter technically capable staff people who understand the business, but almost universally don't understand the character of the customers they attempt to serve. Where it is appropriate, we work through the process inputs and outputs that affect customers and add responsibilities that make employees accountable to customers. In our model, these folks go through the same training regimen as the sales and service people. For roles in areas that do not affect the customer relationship (i.e. finance, HR, legal), we indoctrinate them with the change readiness/sales and service overview workshop and supply them with explicit recommendations to improve the support they provide to the employees that interact with customers.

Senior management must be conscious of a potential pitfall that must be averted as the job reformation process unfolds. Any employees involved in the creation of the new processes begins to recognize that jobs need to change and the personnel skill sets need to be modified or upgraded. As a consequence, it's tempting for these process creators to compare how jobs are performed today versus the future. The customer logic of the new systems becomes tainted quickly and, when one starts exploring how the people fit into the new world, the process suffers even more. Trust us...it's a natural inclination for employees to want to protect colleagues (and themselves) by tweaking things to accommodate the skill sets of the current workforce. Neither of us is inclined to create rules, but in this case we have two principles that we follow with religious conviction:

- *Never* begin to redefine jobs until you have a new baseline process on paper
- *Never* begin to "people" new roles, until we have *approval* on the baseline processes and prototype jobs

Stifle the urge to protect jobs and good things will happen through the logic of the processes.

FORM FOLLOWS FUNCTION

Like architecture, "form ever follows function"[22] is the rallying cry for most organizational design. Companies, small and large, rely on several traditional forms to arrange sales and service resources. Sales divisions tend to organize resources by some combination of: business specialty, product line, location, and/or distribution channel. These classifications are frequently structured around customers, and as a consequence, sales is less likely to require major structural upheaval.

On the other hand, the service organization is normally fashioned to support the internal corporate infrastructure, and not sales or the customers.[23] In fact, most service units are relegated to the default bureaucratic stance, centralization. As a consequence, resources are deployed in departments by job specialty or by professional discipline. As we alluded to in the last section, when jobs are specialized — department functionality follows the same path. [Where there is job specialization, there is also centralization]. Therefore when job responsibilities are consolidated, we look to forms of decentralization and/or multi-functional teams as potential solutions.

To devise a decentralized organizational scheme around the customer, we must retrace our footsteps and answer the question we first posed back in Chapter 3: Who

---

[22] Sullivan, Louis Henry. "The Tall Office Building Artistically Considered." Lippincott's Magazine. March, 1896.

[23] Interestingly, in 1999, Andersen Consulting and the Economist Intelligence Unit co-authored a report entitled "Managing Customer Relationships." They surveyed over 200 senior executives in North America, Europe and Asia. The report indicated that as of 1998 only eighteen (18%) percent of businesses surveyed were organized around customer type.

is the customer? For small and mid-size firms we recommend a monogamous customer relationship, which simplifies the issues around structural change. In more complex organizations, who is the customer must be determined at business unit levels; therefore, expect different units to focus on different customers.

Next validate that the sales structure is properly aligned to the primary customer. In cases where the primary customer is incorrect or where there is some confusion (i.e. there's more than one), the sales structure must be reevaluated. Once the sales configuration is validated or modified, we recommend—as a general rule—aligning direct service functions to the sales side of the business. In other words, take sales and the service employees/units responsible for direct customer interactions, and join them at the hip. Accordingly, if the sales division is structured by product and location, direct service units should be aligned in the same manner.

Then review where customer "points of contact" exist within the new processes and job functions. This can be a tricky balancing act. The first consideration is a matter of structural simplicity. We want a configuration with a certain transparency—one that enables customers to easily reach the right employees. The short answer is a single point of contact. If only things were that straightforward! Complications arise when we wrestle with how far that clarity should go.

Our answer is that businesses need to expand beyond the standard customer herding techniques—especially for their best customers. Dumping a company's "A" customers along with everyone else into the same "box" won't promote loyalty or generate additional sales from this critical segment.

A company must first look to its culture to figure out if

it's acceptable to publicize that "A" customers receive special support. For example, companies that sell a product or service line that symbolizes a customer pecking order (like American Express's credit card categories) are well positioned to differentiate sales and service contact points. Likewise, organizations that encourage a high degree of competitiveness among its customers are also primed for this structural tactic, i.e. a company that considers its independent distributors as the customer. In these instances, our recommendation is to establish a unit responsible for the "A" or first-class customers and another unit charged with servicing everyone else.

Let us be clear. When it is not culturally practical to install a separate unit to support "A" customers, it is not enough for a company to rely exclusively on its systems, policies, and training to provide some sales/service differentiation. Our solution is, in these cases, to deploy multi-functional teams.

The essence of a multi-functional team is to combine sales, direct service and/or indirect service responsibilities together under one unit. Notice the "and/or." When we introduce multi-functional teams into a company, they are a variation on a theme. In some cases, sales and direct service activities are combined into a team. In other companies, the teams are made up of direct and indirect service. And in still others, all three activities are brought together. Now notice the term "responsibilities." Our brand of multi-functional teams doesn't take a handful of staff specialists; lump them under one roof, and call them a team.

> A multi-functional team brings together a group, trained as generalists, to perform a congruent collection of responsibilities.

Don't be lulled into a false sense of security. Having form follow function is an arduous and stressful undertaking. The meetings, the brainstorming, the paper tigers, the meetings, the politicking, and the intense communications all go into putting a new structure in place. It is time-consuming, but vital to the success of the integration model.

There's yet one more angst ridden issue to put on the table: integrating management. When one starts tinkering with middle management fiefdoms, things get...well...real interesting...

MANAGEMENT MUTATIONS

In addition to job reformation and structure redesign, a major outcome of post-integration is fewer management jobs. This reduction in management has averaged close to twenty-five (25%) percent affecting every layer of management without exception. These changes do not come out of the blue. To provide you with format to evaluate management, here is a summary of how we do it.

The discussions begin before we set foot in the company. We have the necessary conversations with the CEO/President and the senior team and gain a general, consensus agreement (based on the collective political will) as to how deep and far-reaching they wish to see change. Once senior management is on board, we meet with the middle managers to discuss what they can expect as the integration process unfolds. We tell this folded armed audience that things will be different. We are open and honest about the fact that there will be fewer management roles. Everyone will be asked to do new things. There will be some wonderful career opportunities for people who are up to the challenge; and, yes, others will ultimately need to make some tough choices. This doesn't necessarily mean managers will not have a job—it means some won't be managing people anymore. Admittedly, this is not the ideal way to win friends and influence people, but subterfuge is the greatest destroyer of the trust we are working to instill.

Fast-forward the scene a few months, and the integration plan—including the recommendations for changes to the management structure—is presented. From a tactical standpoint, we let the logic of the integrated processes, the judiciousness of enriched jobs and the potential of the customer-oriented structure to speak for themselves. The natural changes from integration—the job consolidations, the job responsibilities that are eliminated and added—all contribute to a fresh management landscape.

Up front, we review an organizational chart and a list of job titles/job rankings looking for the obvious anomalies. They're not hard to find. We determine the current number of management levels and calculate a management to staff ratio to get the lay of the land. [We can't stress it enough that both the org chart and the job classifications are necessary. It's common to get an organization chart that shows five or six layers of management; but when we compare that to a listing of management job titles, lo and behold there are seven, eight, maybe even NINE different supervisory rankings].

In particular, warning lights go off whenever we see "Assistant" or "Associate" in front of a supervisory sounding designation–it's usually a tip off for redundancy. We've also found an interesting, somewhat counter-intuitive trend concerning the proportion of managers to staff. Our small/mid-size clients have had a much larger percentage of managers per capita twenty-five (25%) percent to thirty-three (33%) percent compared with larger companies fifteen (15%) percent to twenty (20%) percent.[24]

Once we begin our analysis we look for the less noticeable situations: departments with undersized spans of control, or units where there is a one to one association between a supervisor and manager. We also learn the company's "management lore" by asking inconspicuous questions and listening attentively to the stories of:

- The justifications for pay increases
- The loyalty and longevity promotions
- The "quid pro quo" boosts where one SVP gets his guy or gal a promotion and his/her SVP rival must to do the same
- The got me over a (perceived) barrel, please don't leave, here's more money and a new title scenario, and
- The ever popular "keep the peace" elevations, which comes along with a brand new, supervisory sounding job title

Management types seem to multiply like rabbits — blink — and there's a new managerial role. In the end, integration provides the company with the opportunity to significantly strengthen its ranks.

---

[24] Our figures define a small/mid-size business as one with more than fifty (50) and less than five hundred (500) employees.

Management issues also reach the senior level. There are often departmental changes recommended in the final integration plan that find the corner offices. [We love to live dangerously]. Even the slightest tweak can lead to intense corporate gamesmanship. Here are some examples:

- The plan may call for creating a new unit or two, which must report to a senior manager; and, of course, all of the execs think the new unit(s), should report to them
- We routinely have situations where we need to combine two units (i.e. sales and service), which just happen to be supervised by two different senior managers

While the potential landmines abound, the integration plan must sort out these senior management situations head on. Making judgments about the senior team requires a detailed assessment of each individual's strengths and weaknesses, and an evaluation of the group's overall effectiveness. We look at:

- Individual ability and effectiveness
- Team effectiveness
- Team health

After the assessment, if we conclude that the executive team members most affected by the proposed changes are capable, work well together and are relatively healthy, we will try very hard to fashion win-win scenarios without compromising the integrity of the overall integration plan. If this is not possible or, we determine that there are deficiencies among the senior team (and they can't be easily remedied), this state of affairs forces us to recommend options with clear winners and losers.

Now that we've done all our homework, it's time to present the new management structures to the senior team. Here are a couple of survival tactics:

- Never, ever <u>surprise</u> any members of senior management, regardless of their support/dissent, about jobs, functionality or management structure
- Call things as you see them. If there is even the perception of lost objectivity or of a hidden agenda regarding the management component, it will seriously damage the credibility of the entire plan.

Since the changes to management are just one part of the proposal, we need to describe our recommended actions in the full context of presenting an integration plan:

The Rehearsal. While we are still in the creation stage, during regular project update meetings, we start dropping a few trial balloons (always starting from the bottom-up: processes, jobs, etc.) to the executive sponsor(s). Things are always presented as thoughts and impressions, and we never break our own rules—we don't talk "people." We do the same thing with the president at his/her regular update. Ditto with the other executive decision makers during our seemingly impromptu, "just dropped by to see how things are going..." conversations. We listen, take stock, and reassess (and we do it again and again, with greater intensity and specificity, as we get closer to presenting a final integration blueprint.) Along the way, every executive is figuring things out themselves, making his/her own judgments (as we are) about the ramifications of the ideas. There's no sense in debating things beyond the general reasoning of a brainchild, since some of the ideas will never

143

see the light of day. Remember, the objective to these discussions is to ensure that senior management is not surprised by any of the key employee-related aspects of the integration plan.

Show Time. Having laid the groundwork, start by presenting senior management with the "customer logic"; the sales and service processes, the systems along with a detailed implementation plan to make it happen. Maintain control of the presentation, cover all the hot buttons, and answer anticipated objections before they are raised. After further discussions and some Q&A, present the new organizational design, providing department prototypes and job summaries. Then concentrate on the numbers: the departments added, combined or eliminated and move right into the head count: how staff and management roles are impacted by the proposal. Some staff counts can be a bit vexing (particularly when adding new, untried job responsibilities.) For these, give a best educated range. Finally, present the proposed management reporting lines for first line and middle management only. Make sure they are presented visually — they need to see it immediately. Expect wide-ranging conversations, more Q&A and further clarification of the model. There should be no expectation that any of these plans will be finalized and approved during this session. Then, before ending the meeting, there is a bit of housekeeping to do. With a captive audience, schedule a follow-up session no more than one week later. Also, schedule a meeting with the CEO before the next executive team meeting. The other execs must be forewarned of the discussion, so everything appears transparent and above board.

The Encore. The meeting with the CEO serves two purposes. First, it's an opportunity to take questions and clarify key aspects of the plan. Second, when necessary, it's the time to present him/her with options to restructure senior management (remember visuals.) We can't stress it enough: options are mandatory. When all is said and done, the CEO, and the CEO alone, must make the decisions affecting changes to senior management. If there is only one option, it essentially backs the CEO into a corner—either make the changes or do nothing. Alternatives compel the CEO to consider the circumstances on the merits. And yes, it's now time to talk about the people candidly—strengths and weaknesses—in relationship to the demands of the new roles.

The Critics. In between senior team meetings, it is critical to continue selling the logic (of the new model), solicit feedback from prominent distracters, and listen to (and get answers for) all objections. Informal one-on-one consultations are the best way to accomplish this. Before ever setting foot "on stage," do everything humanly possible to ensure that there is already enough support—the right support—in place for the integration plan to be approved.

The Sequel. This meeting is usually anti-climatic. [In fact, much of the meeting is spent dealing with what's next]. The real work is already done; and a consensus emerges on the vast majority of processes, jobs and structures. Now all the executive team needs to do is give its final seal of approval.

Everything goes according to plan. Sales and service wants the same things with the same urgency and longing as that of new lovers; communicating through "TLC" induces all the pleasures and inspirations of a storybook romance and works with the panache and imagination found in the Kamasutra. Despite this rosy outlook, the initiative can still fail to live up to its billing. Integrating sales and service propels companies to be in the relationship business. It all comes down to people power, since the employees are the real implementers.

CHAPTER 10—PEOPLE INTEGRATION

**Far and away the best prize that life offers is the chance to work hard
at work worth doing.**

*Theodore Roosevelt (**Labor Day speech, 1903**)*

T hroughout this book, we have made several references as to how management should deal with its
employees. Most of the remarks have revolved around
communication issues. We have also reinforced that talk
alone is cheap; management must back up its words with
actions. As a result, what management does, how it treats
employees — in concrete policies and practices — during this
time of transformation ultimately determines the level of
success of integration.

The five people principles we espouse are designed to
maximize management's flexibility while minimizing employee uncertainty:

- Everyone that wants a job in the new world will
  have one
- All jobs that result from integration (new and redefined) will be posted for *anyone* to apply
- Everyone (management and staff) in those areas
  affected by integration must reapply and be inter-
  viewed for the new roles
- When someone is promoted, they will receive an
  applicable salary increase; anyone who accepts a
  position that is considered a demotion will remain

at his or her current salary
- Everyone selected will participate in retraining; everyone will have ample time to assimilate into the new positions

Each of these practices requires a closer examination.

TO LET GO OR NOT

This is the first employee relations question that management must tackle. In our view, you must maintain a delicate balance between using the integration model to change the status quo and using it as a threat to employee security. In other words, integration changes how business is done, but should not be a risk to employee livelihoods. Under normal circumstances streamlining processes, redesigning jobs, and reshaping management—guaranteed outcomes of integration—cause employee insecurity. Employees hear terms like "reengineering" or "restructuring" and translate them into code words for downsizing. We don't want employees to leap to the same conclusion about integration. Building loyalty (customer or employee) requires trust and handing out pink slips is a surefire trustbuster. In our opinion, the collective "psyche" of any business never quite recovers from layoffs.

At one time, executives did everything in their power to avoid layoffs. IBM was as much heralded for its no layoff policy as it was for computer innovation. These days, downsizing is in the mainstream; layoff announcements are literally a daily occurrence. In many management circles, the workforce is viewed as a commodity. Layoffs are employed as the quick and easy cost-reduction tactic of choice. Well, why shouldn't management react this way, when investors reward publicly held corporations that conduct layoffs with near term stock price stability!

Wall Street's hypersensitivity over near term economic prospects and its never ending preoccupation with quarterly profit numbers gives rise to trigger-happy senior executives: miss earnings by a penny and the company's stock price gets hammered. Management needs to show the Street that they're "responsive." They need to improve the financials.[25] The only real deliberations concerns the number of bodies needed to back into the consensus earnings number and how to explain away management's ineptitude.

Small businesses, on the other hand, were less likely to use layoffs (it was akin to terminating kin) but this quasi-taboo has been destroyed as more and more of these businesses also have resorted to staff reductions. There are two rationales for this change in mindset. The quick and dirty answer is monkey see, monkey do. Small businesses are being influenced with what they read and hear in the large corporate sector. There is also merit to the theory that with the rise of venture and vulture capital—many small start-ups are compelled to minimize costs. Labor is a natural place to cut since it represents the largest expense category for most firms.

Back at headquarters middle managers and employees are going berserk. Someone has to figure out who stays and who goes, and this of course must be accomplished without impacting product quality, productivity or servicing

---

[25] In light of all the corporate shenanigans that are being uncovered, "fixin' the financials" has taken on a whole new meaning. Layoffs may not seem so bad, if the only other option is to cook the books! Then the decision comes down to whose trust management wants to shatter. Clearly, corporate stakeholders are experiencing a crisis of confidence with management in general, which only reinforces the need to undertake initiatives, like integration, that focus on building long-term value.

customers. Right. [This is one of the reasons why we recommend downsizing unprofitable clients and getting rid of loss leaders instead]. Employees have responded to this onerous trend in a predictable manner; after all, loyalty is a two-way street. Employees, who were once loyal soldiers who wore their company loyalty like a badge of honor, have been replaced with mercenaries with allegiance only to themselves.

This is why we say layoffs are an absolute last resort and, in fact, in all but one client assignment we have promised employees there would not be layoffs as a result of the integration process. The first time we stand up in front of employees we say, "There will be no layoffs. Jobs will change. New jobs will be created and other jobs will be eliminated. We cannot guarantee that you will be doing the same jobs. Everyone who wants to work in this new, integrated world will have a job..." We're proud that we have never reneged on this pledge.[26] [It's part of the reason why it takes twelve (12) to eighteen (18) months to fully implement an integration plan—and it's why we don't work with firms on the financial brink]. No, we don't advocate a Japanese lifetime employment model. We apply sound, sensible workforce management practices.

To this end, immediately:

---

[26] We have only one client where this promise could not be made to the staff. In this case we told the staff that "it is not our hope or intent that layoffs will result from the initiative; but, we cannot guarantee there will not be layoffs."

- Implement a hiring freeze during the review stage on those jobs/unit most likely to be affected by integration, and
- Institute targeted reductions for non-essential operating expenses

Both steps are preemptive strikes. Reducing operating expenses up front is a way to cushion the blow of lost productivity while the staff is being retrained later in the process. The hiring freeze is based on a "pay me now, pay me later" adage. The company absorbs some normal staff reductions due to attrition or performance problems, so they do not face the possibility of laying those folks off later. Depending upon normal attrition rates, the company may reach a point where other interim steps are necessary to keep things going. If this occurs:

- *Cross train and reallocate resources.* In several situations we have instituted cross training initiatives and shifted resources into units with the most urgent staffing needs. [We're far enough along in the process to have a good idea which areas will be impacted by integration, so we target those people first].
- *Implement easy "blockbuster" process efficiencies right away.* If fortunate enough to devise a new process that does not require a lot of preparation work and it will have a dramatic impact on staff productivity—train and introduce the new process sooner than later.

These stopgap solutions are designed to buy some time and they usually do the trick.

PREPARING FOR CHAOS

Chaos Theory, attributed to the French mathematician Henri Poincaré, describes the unpredictable nature of systems that are sensitive to their starting positions. Scientists once believed by eliminating random influences, chaos, or system variably could be eliminated. We now know that two identical chaotic systems, each set in motion from slightly different starting conditions, can quickly produce different results. Implementing the staffing plan is an exercise in chaos theory. Our "starting position" is a blank sheet of paper. Now consider our desired outcomes (the random influences at work):

- We want the best people in the right jobs
- Every new and every redefined job is posted
- Anyone in the organization can apply
- No exceptions

Before management ever sets foot in front the podium to announce the restructuring plan, they need to do some prep work. It's the only medicine to maintain a sense of control over the coming upheaval.

Senior management must fine-tune the dimensions of the staffing plan by taking the proposed integration staffing numbers and weighing them against the firm's historical averages for employee turnover (attrition and normal retirement), the current temporary/contract workforce and staff overtime figures. If the data is available, these projections should be fine-tuned down to the level of job classification. These figures tell management whether staffing factors will help or hurt the cause, and they provide a basis for determining the most effective workforce management tactics. For example, we produced a staffing plan for one client that necessitated a fifteen (15%) percent reduction in current staffing levels. The company's employee turnover rate, across the board, was less than five (5%) percent and the company was too young to count on help from retirements. Our saving grace turned out to be the firm's pervasive use of temporary workers and overtime. Another client's plan called for close to a twenty (20%) percent staff reduction. Its overall employee turnover rate was running at about the same level. At first blush we thought this would be a great help; however, when we looked at the roles most affected by the plan we found two troubling historical trends: turnover for the lower skilled specialists (most of the jobs targeted for elimination) was less than ten (10%) percent; turnover for higher skilled specialists (enriched positions slated for expansion) was about one (1) in three (3). In this case, we suspect the combination of improved job prospects internally and an economic downturn caused turnover to decelerate among the higher skilled workers. A heavy dose of retraining was enough to maintain staffing continuity with the less skilled.

Management must also create an employee selection process that is sensitive to widespread employee uncertainty. The first time employees hear that jobs will change; they blow it off. [Most folks don't believe the initiative will ever get off the ground so there's no sense getting all worked up over things]. As the integration process moves forward, however, anxiety levels heighten. By the time management is ready to announce the new jobs and new organizational structure, employees are probably at the boiling point. They know the stakes are high for the entire company.

We recognize that some of the uncertainty is attributable to our policies. Advocating the "rehire" of managers and staff is the obvious culprit. While the intent is to give management the ability to assemble the best available talent, there are also positives for employees. Many folks are offered new career opportunities: promotions, more satisfying jobs and higher pay. On the other hand, we're dealing with people's livelihoods and a host of self-worth issues. Making reassurances about no layoffs and reinforcing the no salary decrease policy, does help to mitigate the livelihood issues, but that alone cannot sooth egos.

The selection process cannot become a game of "horse trading." If management resorts to any appearance of deal making, it will only reinforce any lingering negative trust issues over its intentions and place a black cloud over the entire initiative. This must be a very public undertaking. It's the only way to combat the trust factor; and when things are executed well, it will put the integration initiative on a solid foundation. The company must do everything in its power to create a process that ensures respect, fairness and transparency. Here's how to do it:

First, we advise against any prescreening (no one gets rejected out of hand.) When everyone gets an initial interview, a level playing field is maintained.

Second, we advocate a selection committee for middle management and staff jobs. Don't get us wrong — we don't look for ways to complicate matters — our eyes are on ensuring fairness and openness. We're just realists. By using a selection committee the voices spanning the company's political spectrum have the opportunity to be heard. This committee should not have more than three managers — the manager to whom the successful candidates will report, the executive sponsor and one other good judge of management talent.

Third, devise a realistic assignment related to integration that all management applicants must prepare. We have had candidates draft a business plan based on the new integration model. It was a tremendous eye opener for spotting budding management talent (and the lack thereof within the existing management ranks.)

Fourth, don't deviate from the announced process (unless management wants to fight a round of stories about job predetermination.)

Lastly, management must be prepared to communicate all selection decisions to employees face-to-face.

There are also procedural considerations:

- There needs to be a job posting schedule. Management jobs should be posted first (so employees know upfront for whom they may be working)
- Determine the materials employees need to submit when they apply (i.e. a resume or some type of work summary)
- Have job descriptions prepared and available for all employees ahead of time, and modify (or create) hiring criteria for the affected jobs
- Hold a job fair staffed by the people who know the jobs best to give employees a personal perspective about the work (it's also a great opportunity to sell the merits of integration)
- Encourage people to apply for multiple roles and maybe even to throw their hat into the ring for a more challenging position

By attending to these matters before hand, management will ease some of the uncertainty and gain some credibility at the same time.

IN THE MIST

The outcome of the selection process is—not surprising — a real mixed bag. Some jobs can be filled easily with top-notch talent. Other positions will necessitate taking a few chances, and still other positions fall in the "no way in hell" category, which will necessitate hiring from the outside. Identify those anticipated hard to fill jobs early in the process, so the company can start outside recruiting activities. However, we strongly advise against pulling the trigger on any external candidates, because there may be some pleasant surprises from the internal selection process.

We guarantee the interview process will alter long held beliefs about the talents of some employees. Expect to find some hidden gems — employees with long forgotten skills or past experiences well suited for an integrated world. Also expect to see a number people who are worth taking a chance on in "stretch" positions. Take those chances. There is no downside. The success stories are irreplaceable loyalty builders. Alas, there will also be unintended consequences and some real difficult decisions for you to make.

Management must maintain a delicate balance between identifying the "keepers" while not succumbing to unreasonable employee "demands" that bastardize the hiring process. There is no room for sacred cows or management pets of any species. There are three employee segments (usually long-term folks) where these situations are most likely to occur: "working" managers, those working in "niche" jobs and/or those with "attitudes."

Our general rules of thumb for handling these individuals need no explanation:

- No one is irreplaceable
- Use common sense
- Don't enable inappropriate behavior
- Never be held hostage

After that, these employees need to be dealt with on a case-by-case basis. Let's get employee attitudes out of the way. The solution is clear-cut and it provides the script for any employees who have the unenviable distinction of falling into more than one "problem" category. Here's how we draw the line.

Is the employee's attitude a display of a pessimistic or cynical outlook? Or, is the attitude a symptom of more destructive behavior? Employees that see the world as half empty, the naturally distrusting and sarcastic, but otherwise productive employees, are generally worth saving. Their grousing may be a pain; but they also tend to be some of the most loyal and hard working employees around. It's our experience that once these "doubting Thomases" see integration working, they get the religion and convert other like-minded skeptics. We define people with destructive tendencies as those who resist change overtly through open defiance or other inappropriate actions — these folks dig in their heels and treat any change to the status quo as if it were Custer's Last Stand. They choose to fight by not applying for any new jobs or by making extraordinary and unrealistic demands of management — with an "or else" thrown in for effect. If multiple attempts to reach a rational solution fail, take them up on the "or else."

The new management structure causes fewer chiefs, changes the political landscape and heightens performance standards. In addition to a greater degree of accountability and larger spans of control, our model stresses that managers manage full-time. Even the most corporate-like organization has its share of bosses who were promoted into management because they were good technicians. Some turn into fine supervisors, while others...well, let's just say the Peter Principle, not to mention The Dilbert Principle, is

alive and well. Yet, we see more numbers and higher rank-
ing working managers/manager technicians in firms that
have a strong entrepreneurial history. In these organizations, work output tends to have a greater value than managing people.

Unless the business suffers from a real talent deficiency,
sorting through the ranks to recognize the best people for
management is not too difficult. Be objective about a person's past results. Raise the bar. Gauge future performance.
Don't make excuses. Have the political courage to make the
right selection decisions:

- *Remove the clear underachieving managers.* Transfer
  these folks back into roles where they were successful in the past or into a position that leverages
  their talents.
- *Give the mediocre middles one last shot.* Provide individual support (i.e. mentoring, training) to help
  them succeed, but make it unmistakably clear that
  if they don't produce, they're out.
- *Elevate/prepare legitimate management up and comers.*
  There may be an opportunity to promote a real
  star. If this is not possible, start training management prospects now. Send these people to an in-
  troductory management workshop and find other
  development opportunities so when there is a future management opening, the company has a
  cadre of talented understudies waiting in the
  wings.

There is little tangible difference in the outcomes with
the staff selections — there is no way management can make
everybody happy. You should solicit the opinions of direct
supervisors during the selection process; however, it is un-

realistic for them to have final decision making authority. One's own self-interest prevents them from being completely objective. The selection committee must distribute the talents and personalities equally among the operating units. Without getting into too much detail, every department should have its share of stars, steady-eddies and under achievers. Look for employees with complimentary skills to strengthen the whole team. Be conscious of each manager's abilities—we want them to succeed. For example, try to give the stretch manager a strong number two. Avoid giving a new manager or weak manager a problem employee they are not ready to handle. Also, distribute staff keeping an eye on the exits. If someone has checked out mentally, consider the staffing complement assuming that person is preparing to check out physically. Speaking of checking out...

We take a straightforward approach to handling employee performance issues during this time of upheaval. Every new manager reviews the personnel files to familiarize themselves with employee work records. All current disciplinary action is transferred along with the employee to the new manager. We advise those managers to informally counsel the employee, telling them that this is the perfect opportunity to turn their performance around, but we strongly advise against using this occasion to address long ignored problems. Communicate expectations to everyone. If a performance issue rears its ugly head, counsel and provide reasonable support. If things don't improve, suck it up and do what needs to be done. Events will occur that require management to adjust and fine-tune the staffing complement, but management must be patient. Give people time to get comfortable with the new, integrated world of sales and service.

THE COMMITMENT TO JOB RETRAINING

The way to make certain employees have the best chance for success is for management to commit fully to job retraining. Thus far, most of our commentary regarding training has focused on improving employee sales and service skills. Job retraining is equally important to the success of the program. The changes to forms, manual work processes, and computer applications combined with the expanded scope of jobs, necessitates that employees relearn everyday tasks. The level of training will clearly correspond with the extent of the work and job modifications. The time and effort required to design a job retraining program is contingent upon how well (or how poorly) the company trained new employees in the past and whether or not the company has experienced trainers on staff. Here are the major prerequisites for a successful program:

- *Full-time trainer(s).* Pulling together a proficient program is not something that can be accomplished on a part-time basis. If the firm does not have experienced trainers, the initial work can be outsourced; however, in the long-term we recommend sending several people who have displayed the innate skills (good writers, stand-up communicators, and/or job experts) to a train the trainer program.
- *Space.* A dedicated area (at least temporarily) with decent audio/visual capabilities. A computer and LCD projector (if computer work is involved) and an easel is all one really needs.
- *Detailed process documentation.* We mean more than flow-charts. Clear and precise *written*, step-by-step instructions, complete with decision trees, are necessary. Copies of all forms and computer screens

employees will utilize must be included in the document as well.

- *Experiential design.* Adults learn by doing. The program must be engaging and relevant. Employees need to work with the same tools they will work with on the job.
- *Collect background knowledge (e.g. company, industry, technology, etc.)* This is essential particularly for businesses that had many people working as specialists. Don't make the mistake of assuming employees understand the company's business or the industry in which they work. If our experiences are any indication, employees are misinformed or don't know the basics about the business.
- *Availability of individual coaching.* Whether it's the manager mentoring or the training staff doing some refresher work, some employees may need more hand holding to get up to speed.

The commitment management makes to job retraining now has a lasting impact on current and future employee performance.

EPILOGUE—ENDURING AFTERGLOW

Patience and tenacity of purpose are worth more than twice their weight of cleverness.

Thomas Henry Huxley (Collected Essays, 1893.)

I t would be nirvana if every time a customer deals with your organization they come away from the encounter feeling the same warmth, that lighter than air bounce and utter rapture as they do after experiencing an overpowering, breathtaking sunset. [It is, after all, the literal meaning of "afterglow"]. To achieve our version of 'enduring afterglow,' the principles of integrating sales and service must become the way the company does business. Perpetuating customer relationships to acquire new customers, to build loyalty and to cultivate additional sales, are attained when integration behaviors become the "norm." It requires time.

It seems, however, that every new management scheme that comes along these days is branded with such hyperbole it's as if the ideas are the Holy Grail of business commerce—holding an elixir so powerful that it is guaranteed to cure the ills of any company—quickly and easily. These business solutions are neatly packaged into smart buzzwords cleverly labeled as paradigms, principles or other snappy terms. What choice do the gurus have when the work world demands sound byte stratagems and branded "infotainment" with a short-term outlook?

There are many smart people providing top-notch services, but there are also plenty of charlatans peddling junk. These throw away initiatives are launched with great fanfare right out of the pages of a Hollywood premiere complete with speeches, animated PowerPoint presentations, photo ops, and food. These "experts" come to preach wherever there's a captive audience. They sermonize during meetings, brainstorming sessions and training workshops. They even lecture in the restrooms during breaks. Employees leave these "feel good" events rejuvenated, happily regurgitating the program lingo at the slightest hint of a politically opportune moment. Then inexplicably the air goes out of the balloon...

Sometimes the balloon just bursts and the program is quickly abandoned. The management team realizes there was a lot of style and no substance. Other times the air leaks out slowly. In these instances, the program's demise is usually traced to methodologies that are so exhaustive the real work of the company suffers. In the end, how and why is irrelevant; results were not delivered as promised.

We don't want any integration initiative to endure that same fate.

We are upfront about the fact that integrating sales and service is not a quick fix program. Trust us, we are not being self-righteous saying so. To be honest, we struggled mightily over the notion that our solutions should be quick and easy. Some time ago, we even toyed with designing an "Integration Lite" to answer the time objection. In the end, we both agreed not to scale things back. We would become the very snake oil consultant types we so despise by promising things we couldn't deliver. Twelve to eighteen months is not too long when a company is in business for the long haul.

There comes a time when words ring hollow. We're at that point. It's time to act. Integrate sales and service. Your customers and your bottom line will see the difference.

To Share *Integrating Sales and Service* with a "CellMate"

Individual or bulk copies of the book can be ordered on-line at www.cbsg.com or www.virtualbookworm.com.

For "Integrating Sales and Service" consulting, training programs and learning product information:
Telephone 888-411-5800 or visit www.cbsg.com